THE HEALING POWER
OF CHRIST

THE

HEALING POWER

OF CHRIST

by Emily Gardiner Neal

HAWTHORN BOOKS, INC.
W. Clement Stone, Publisher
New York

Library of Congress Card Number: 70-179121
ISBN: 0-8015-3348-1

Designed by Martin J. Baumann

4 5 6 7 8 9 10

The scriptural passages quoted in this book are from the King James version unless otherwise noted. The abbreviations of other translations are as follows:

B.C.P.	Book of Common Prayer
Jer.	Jerusalem Bible
N.E.B.	New English Bible
Phillips	Phillips translation
R.S.V.	Revised Standard Version

This book, written for the glory of God, is dedicated to the Reverend Donald Turley James, great Christian, faithful Episcopal priest, and beloved friend.

Foreword

MY FIRST BOOK, *A Reporter Finds God*,[1] conceived when I was an agnostic, was intended to be an exposé of "faith healing." As I researched the subject, however, I was myself converted, and the book was to end as an apologetic for the Christian faith in general and the healing ministry in particular.

Since that first book, others have followed as I have watched the ministry of healing spread from what, just a few years ago, was considered an esoteric practice, confined to a few churches (mostly Episcopal) to hundreds of churches of virtually every denomination. In these churches it is acknowledged for what it is: a scripturally founded ministry following the commandment of our Lord to preach the kingdom *and* heal the sick (Luke 9:2). It is a ministry that accepts Jesus' revelation of a God who wills the complete wholeness of body, mind, and spirit for His children; a ministry practiced by the ancient church in obedience to Christ's imperative; a ministry that almost died out after the third century; a ministry that has been revived today and in which we see manifested much of the spiritual power of the early church as we observe ailing bodies marvelously healed and sick spirits restored to wholeness.

Over the past years I have become increasingly in-

[1] New York: Morehouse-Gorham, 1956.

volved in the ministry of healing until it now consumes
not just a major portion of my time, but my entire life.
I have led innumerable healing missions in churches of
every denomination throughout the United States and
Canada, and only lack of time has prevented my accepting invitations to Europe and Australia.

Since 1966, at the invitation of the rector, the Reverend
Dr. John Baiz, and with the permission of my bishop, I
have had the privilege of leading weekly interdenomina-
tional healing services at Calvary Episcopal Church in
Pittsburgh. These are always conducted in participation
with a clergyman. Believing as I do that the healing
ministry must be kept within the church if it is to be pro-
tected from chicanery and the excesses of misplaced zeal,
I work always under the authority of my church. As my
deepest desire and chief purpose is to see the establish-
ment of healing ministries in every church, the work at
Calvary has been enormously gratifying, for as a result of
these weekly services, numerous clergy of different denominations have begun healing services in their own
churches.

More healings are occurring today than at any time
since I have been associated with this ministry. This is
particularly evident in regard to cases of acute leukemia.
For years it was virtually impossible to procure reliable
documentation of this disease. Over the past few years at
Calvary and during missions, I have seen numbers of
such cases diagnosed as "acute" where the life expectancy
was estimated to be very short regardless of possible
remissions and the administration of new drugs.

By means of concentrated prayer, the sacramental healing rites, and holy communion, remissions have occurred,
many of them of such long duration that it seems reasonable to suppose that cures have been effected. In my
experience the reception of holy communion in this disease—and indeed in all blood disorders—is of supreme

importance. There is a close relationship between the
Blood of Christ shed for us and that received by us in
this sacrament, cleansing, healing, and mystically cours-
ing through the veins of the supplicant. No matter how
young the leukemia victim, I urge frequent communions.

In ever increasing number we see the crippled walk,
the blind see, and the deaf hear. We see the retarded
restored to normalcy, the emotionally and mentally sick
healed. We see brokenness of all kinds, in every area of
life, healed. And in the area of unbelief, which constitutes
the greatest of all brokenness, we see the greatest of all
miracles as the faithless are brought to Christ.

"Hitherto have ye asked nothing in my name," Jesus
says. "Ask and ye shall receive, that your joy may be full"
(John 16:24). We have asked, we have received, and we
know well that joy of which He speaks.

As you will note throughout this book, the healing
ministry is in no way confined to physical illness; it
touches every area of our lives. The healing Christ extends
His hand to bless, to heal, to bring us to Him. The ministry of healing, although only one of the ministries of
the church, serves in unique fashion to open our hearts
to the love of God. At the altar rails of the healing church,
Christ is overwhelmingly present, and there is an almost
startling awareness of Himself and of His love which *is*
Himself. It is this awareness that enables us to meet and
conquer two of the major problems confronting not only
our youth but individuals of every age: the apparent
meaninglessness of life and the agonizing search for
self-identity.

As we discover with impelling impact through the healing ministry that Christ does indeed live today, we find
in Him the meaning of our lives. In our subsequent commitment to Him we find new purpose, for we know at
last the reason for our being. In regard to the so-called
identity crisis, we recall the words of Saint Augustine:

"Let me know Thee, Lord, and let me know myself." It is in knowing God that we come to know ourselves as His children. For me and for many, this is enough. We know at last who we are and why. Our search is ended. We are found.

Properly understood, the healing ministry is not a ministry of self-gratification. It extends far beyond the needs of the individual or those close to him. It involves itself deeply in the world's suffering. Those associated with this ministry do not dwell in ivory towers. They attempt to follow the precepts of our Lord, fully aware that they are His hands and feet in this world, cognizant that as the body without the spirit is dead, so faith without works is also dead (James 2:26).

This book is the continuing story of the healing Christ at work among us today as surely as he was present among the people two thousand years ago. It tells of some of the marvelous healings of every kind in the lives of twentieth-century men, women, and children. In order to avoid what might be an undesirable identification with any particular church or mission, I have intentionally "scrambled" the healings and other happenings recorded. For example, where one particular episode occurred which could be identified with one particular mission, I have included in this same mission, stories and case histories which in fact occurred elsewhere—many of them at Calvary in Pittsburgh. The important thing is that everything reported happened under the circumstances described.

As the book relates wonderful healings wrought by God, so does it tell of the no less wonderful way in which He uses suffering as we await our healing. Suffering as well as healing is now rooted in my own experience, and it is the sharing of this suffering that makes this book unusual. Many people actively engaged in the healing ministry attempt to keep knowledge of their illnesses from the public, no doubt feeling that if it is generally known that they have not received instantaneous healing, the faith of others in the healing Christ may be damaged. From my observations, I do not believe this to be true. On the contrary, I have seen the hope and faith of the vast majority strengthened when they learn that even a leader in the healing field is not always immediately physically cured, but that in the strength of Christ he is enabled to go on in the unshakable conviction of God's will and power to heal.

For years I felt presumptuous when from the pinnacle of my own extraordinarily good health I would say to the suffering, " 'Seek ye *first* the Kingdom' is the master key to healing. You must seek God for Himself and not just His healing gifts. Therein lies your best hope of physical healing." I no longer feel presumptuous in saying these words, and I know their validity as I never fully understood before. I have had to apply them to myself, because for a period of nearly six years I was never a day without pain, and had it not been for the strength of Christ in which I walked and worked, I would have been totally incapacitated from a spinal injury suffered in 1965. Although for years there was no evidence of healing in my own body, I feel myself not less blessed, but more—for I have known His grace in my life to an extent I never knew before, continually sustaining, enabling and empowering.

While I no longer feel hesitant in asking the suffering to seek God for himself alone, I do not underestimate the difficulty of this undertaking. I realize that there are times when pain supersedes all else; but I also know that there are times when the pain, no matter what the ailment, is less. God in His mercy requires only a moment of complete relinquishment to Him to work a miracle.

Some of my beloved friends, without whose prayers I could not have continued, have said to me in real dis-

tress, "But why should *you* have to suffer so?" Deeply
grateful for their concern, I was nevertheless upset myself
by this question because they were upset. The answer
seemed to me so clear: Why *not* I? Everyone on earth is
subject to suffering, and why should I be immune? To
be a Christian is not an insurance policy against the coming of disaster; it is rather assurance against being overcome by it—for no matter what happens to us, we hold in
our hearts the joy of the Lord, submerged at times by
pain or adversity, but always deep within our beings. We
may indeed suffer, but He was crucified and yet rose
again. No matter what happens to us, we know that beyond the Cross lies the Resurrection. In this knowledge
lies that joy which cannot be taken from us.

It seems to me a sort of blasphemy to castigate God by
the querulous question, "Why?" It is only when we learn
to stop this needless questioning that we feel impelled
to offer Him endless praise and thanksgiving simply because He lives and because we know it; because He is
with us and within us every second of the day and night;
because He heals, and we experience His healing; because
He loves, and we are the objects of His love; because
with Him all things are possible, and *in* Him lies our
hope, our joy, the reason for our being.

I have been blessed by my friends and am grateful
beyond the telling for their love, concern, and ceaseless
prayer. I have been deeply moved and inexpressibly
thankful when during many missions and at the Calvary
services total strangers learning of my physical difficulty
have surrounded and upheld me by prayer.

I thank God for my Christian family physician, for his
medical skill and for his belief in the power of prayer.
Throughout the years he never relinquished hope of my
healing, despite the verdict of orthopedists, neurosur-
geons, and doctors of physical medicine, whose common
opinion was that I should stop working and learn to live

"with a physical condition which in all probability would worsen with time."

Finally, no words of mine can adequately express my gratitude to God for the late Reverend Donald T. James, director of the Pittsburgh Experiment, who ministered to me faithfully as I struggled to keep going. He gave unstintingly of that love, divinely bestowed, which he possessed to so extraordinary a degree. And God worked through him to heal in the way that mattered most.

At the end, Don was to give me the gift I treasure above all others in this world: the privilege of ministering to him after his first heart attack. The year following was one of mutual ministration for which I shall always be grateful: a year of joy, of healing, of singular closeness to one of the great Christians of our time.

"Call unto me, and I will answer thee, and show thee great and mighty things, which thou knowest not" (Jer. 33:3). This is the promise magnificently fulfilled in His ministry of healing.

E.G.N.

Contents

"By the bruising of my whole life, strengthen me with sympathy for every wounded soul, and let my prayers be as balm for the wounds of Thy children, that they may be healed."
—Dorothy Kerin, *Called by Christ to Heal*

Chapter 1

THE LONG ROAD BEGINS

GLANCING AT MY watch, I noted that within half an hour the plane would be arriving at my destination—a city far from home—where I was to lead a three-day healing mission. The stewardess was serving coffee to the passengers, when the plane hit rough weather. I smiled to myself at the seemingly inevitable simultaneity of air pockets and coffee-serving. As the "Fasten Seat Belt" sign flashed on, I started to reach out for my cup but quickly changed my mind. The plane was pitching and plunging too much to risk a shower of hot coffee. The stewardess, undaunted, walked past me, struggling to keep her balance.

As the plane hit another air pocket I tightened my seat belt, and at that moment a small child, sitting a few seats in front of me, escaped from his parents and began to run up the aisle. The plane gave a lurch and the child started to fall. Instinctively I twisted quickly in my seat to catch him. That sudden movement of my body, confined as it was by the seat belt, wrenched my back in such searing pain that I thought I would faint.

At the time of the initial injury to my back, six months earlier, I had had to cancel one mission, fortunately the last of that season and the first I had ever had to cancel. It had been a difficult summer of lying flat on my back for weeks on end, but by the grace of God I was up and around once more, and had recently completed several missions. As I sat in my plane seat now in excruciating pain, I could only pray; "Lord, if I am to do this mission, You'll have to make it possible."

The plane landed, and with superhuman effort I got myself down the ramp, where I was met by the smiling rector of the mission church, who was full of plans for the mission which was to begin the next day. I said nothing about my back until we arrived at the hotel where I was to stay. Unable to get out of the car, I was forced to tell him what had happened.

I will long remember his kindness. Instead of being upset over the probable cancellation of the event planned two years before and widely publicized, his sole concern was for me. After a short prayer, he called a physician who, after a cursory examination, said that I must be hospitalized at once.

"But what about the mission?" I asked.

"Forget it," was the response. But this was an unrealistic order, for how could I "forget" it when I knew that busloads of people were arriving from far-distant points, that hundreds would be bitterly disappointed, and that there was no time to procure another missioner?

Early next morning while I was still groggy from Demerol, the physician and rector stopped by my hospital room. Before either could speak, I said, "I'll do the mission." The physician demurred but was understanding albeit skeptical.

"All right," he said, "if you think you can. But of course you'll have to return to the hospital immediately after each session. Have therapy as often as possible, and we'll try to keep you free from pain."

An hour before I was to leave for the church for the opening service that evening, three nurses came in to dress me. A back brace had been hastily fitted, and while one nurse was strapping me into it as I lay on the bed, another was pulling on my stockings. The third nurse stood by my head and said, "Mrs. Neal, please don't try it. You'll never make it."

I knew better than anyone that I could never make it on my own—but I also knew that I could "do all things through Christ which strengtheneth me" (Phil. 4:13).

When I was finally dressed but still lying flat, the physician came in with a packet of pain pills. "Take one of these now," he said, "and carry the others with you. You can sneak one into your mouth as you take a sip of water from the pulpit."

I refused the pills, afraid to take them lest they befuddle my mind, and the physician left the room.

To my surprise and joy, the nurses stood around my bed, and one of them said, "We'd like to pray for you before you go." Deeply grateful and greatly strengthened, I managed to get off the bed, and I was taken to the church.

As I stepped into the pulpit, the first person I saw was the kind physician, who had taken time off to come to the service; he was waiting to catch me if I fell. However, stronger hands than his were to hold me up that night.

The church was packed, and only the rector and I were to administer the laying on of hands. According to usual custom we divided the altar rail, he taking one half and I the other.

The line of people streaming up to receive the healing rite seemed endless. Each time I finished my section of the rail, I turned toward the altar with the silent prayer, "Lord, let Thy strength be made perfect in my weakness." Little did I know that night that this would be the burden of my prayer for years to come, as during mission after mission I could not under my own power stand on my feet.

By the time the last group came up to receive the laying on of hands, I had been standing for nearly four hours, and I could scarcely walk. Reaching down to hang on to the altar rail, I suddenly felt a firm hand under my left elbow and then an arm around my waist, which held me up straight and strong until the last supplicant had been ministered to. The service over, I slipped out the back door and into the waiting car which returned me to the hospital.

Next morning the rector telephoned and I thanked him for supporting me at the rail the night before. With some embarrassment I felt compelled to add, "I certainly needed your help last evening, as I was about to collapse, but tonight could you please get us more clergy to help with the laying on of hands? I managed last night because you held me up and I am grateful, but please don't do it again. It seems hardly suitable at a formal service to have you with your arm around me supporting me!"

There was a long silence at the other end of the telephone—and then, in a small voice, came his words: "Emily, I didn't touch you during that service. I was finished before you, and during the last fifteen minutes I was kneeling before the high altar."

Then I knew: Not only had Christ upheld me, He had quite literally held me up. And so it was to be in the years that lay ahead. At home I was unable to stand for the reading of a psalm, but during a mission I was on my feet for three or four hours at a time, solely in His strength.

During this mission there was a great outpouring of the Holy Spirit, and many healings were reported. The only obligation I could not fulfill was that of greeting people after the services. If the time between the various daytime sessions was short, the rector would take me to his study, where with the door locked I lay on the floor (my back needed a hard surface) until time for the next event. Again, little did I know that for months and years to come, I would have to rest on the floor of the clergyman's study in whose church the mission was being held. I am sure my record is unique in one respect at least: Never has anyone lain on the floors of so many pastors' studies!

I was in the hospital for some days after the mission, during which time several prayer-group members came to visit me. This was a surprise, as I was unaware that anyone other than the clergy knew I was there. As I look back now, it was actually these kind women who sowed the first seeds for this book. One said to me, "Why didn't you let us know your predicament so we could have been praying for you?" My only answer was the true one: It had never occurred to me to tell these people, and I could only wonder why it had not.

The love and concern of these prayer-group members, and the letters I received later, demonstrated once again how God can use any and everything for His glory. Typical of these letters was one which read: "I was miserably ill last week—and then I remembered your doing that mission in the strength of Christ. What an inspiration, as through you we saw the living Christ sustain and enable. Suddenly my own sickness seemed very trivial, and God healed me in record time."

It was recalling letters like this that caused me to believe that for others as well as myself the visible evidence of the enabling power of the Holy Spirit was as great a miracle as a physical healing.

Before leaving the hospital, the physicians urged me to cancel missions scheduled for the immediate future.

Rather than canceling them, I rescheduled them for the following fall and winter. This made an exceedingly heavy schedule for the year ahead. I did not dream that I would not be perfectly well by then. Yet, despite frequent further injury, by God's grace I have never had to cancel or even curtail another mission—nor have I ever been obliged to miss a healing service at Calvary.

On the basis of my own experience, I am amused as I think of the lengths to which many of us who work in the healing ministry go in our attempts to explain away Saint Paul's thorn in the flesh (II Cor. 12:7).

I myself have done this often, both in former books and in public speaking, for in years gone by, people would often ask: "But what about Paul's thorn? If *he* wasn't healed, how can *I* expect to be?"

The answer I invariably gave was, first, no one really knows what the apostle's thorn was. The phrase is used in three other places in the Bible (Num. 33:55; Jos. 23:13; Judges 2:3), and in no case does it relate to physical illness. Therefore Paul's thorn may well have referred not to a physical infirmity but to a spiritual one, such as pride.

Whatever Paul's thorn, it was apparently eventually healed, for in Gal. 4:13 his infirmity is referred to in the past tense.

All this is true. However, when people occasionally still say to me: "But what about Paul's thorn in the flesh?" my reply is: "Well, what about it?" It seems to me now to matter not at all. There are only two things in connection with it which seem of importance:

First, whatever it was, it was not of God. "There was given me a thorn in the flesh, the messenger of Satan to buffet me," Paul says (II Cor. 12:7).

Second, the all-importance of God's answer to Paul when he prayed that the thorn be removed: "My grace is sufficient for thee, for my strength is made perfect in weakness" (II Cor. 12:9). And so it was. The apostle was enabled to do the will of God and in the process to endure stonings, shipwreck, and persecution. No matter what Paul suffered, it did not impede his work, for Christ was always victorious.

So it was during this mission led from the hospital, and so it would be in all the missions to come for a long, long time. I thought often of St. Paul, and drew courage from his example.

There was not a day during these years that I did not expect and claim the miracle of physical healing in my own life. As time after time I received the healing rites, at a point at which I felt I could bear no more suffering, the pain would marvelously cease. I would be certain then that the healing had occurred—and so, for the moment, it had. But for reasons I did not know, I could not hold it. Within a short while, the pain would be back; but it was as if by each easement of the pain God was reassuring me of His mercy and love. As a result, I never for a single moment at any time felt abandoned by Him, and I was more sure than ever before of His will to heal.

Nevertheless, there was so much I wanted to do in Christ's service which was now impossible that at times I felt almost overwhelmed by frustration. During one such time I was reading Scripture, and Elisha's words to Elijah leaped from the page: "I pray thee, let a double portion of thy spirit be upon me" (II Kings 2:9).

Closing my Bible, I pondered these words, puzzled why they should seem meaningful, since within the context of the passage in which they occurred there was certainly no possible personal application. Still wondering, I reopened the Bible at random, and my eyes fell upon the words, "They shall possess the double: everlasting joy shall be unto them" (Isa. 61:7).

Suddenly a great light shone: Impressed upon my heart was the conviction that the Lord rewards those who are afflicted, by a double portion of His Spirit. This, then, was the secret of the supernatural strength and grace which were mine, making the impossible possible. "I declare that I will render double unto thee" (Zech. 9:12). He has—and my gratitude, as my joy, is everlasting.

Through it all—the long hours spent in bed lying perfectly flat, unable to read because holding even a paperback book caused painful strain on the back; the months that ran into years during which I could be up only four hours at a time—I was to learn much by the teaching of the Spirit, much of prayer, and what it meant to be alone with God. And I was to learn that whatever *He* wanted me to do, He would make possible, and that which I thought I should be doing was often not at all necessary. That I have been able to continue to work and have never had to cancel a mission since that first hospitalization has been the continuing and marvelous evidence of the power of the Holy Spirit.

I was to learn what it was to be stripped of pride—so often, between connecting planes, I would be forced to lie down in airport waiting rooms, and on many occasions, on the floor of the airport's ladies' lounge.

I was to learn patience—and this in itself was a minor miracle, for by temperament I am impatient, hard-driving, hard-working, and filled with energy.

I was to learn a new compassion for all who suffer, for one who has not himself suffered cannot possibly fully comprehend it.

I was to learn experientially the validity of what I have so long taught: that when one is healed in spirit, the healing of the body is no longer of primary importance. Thus when people would say accusingly, "Why don't you ever speak of your back?" I could honestly reply, "Why should I? It's not that important."

Many have asked me how I became personally involved with the healing ministry. Let me begin by saying that probably no one is more surprised than I at the life I find myself leading. It has been a perfect illustration of what our Lord meant when He said, "Ye have not chosen me, but I have chosen you" (John 15:16). That He has seen fit to choose me to work in His ministry is just another example of the unlikely people He selects to work in His name.

God has given us free will to accept or reject Him, but although He has given us perfect freedom in His service, a curious paradox asserts itself: He draws us to Himself not by force, but nonetheless inexorably by love. This is precisely what happened to me.

As both my parents were atheists, I received no religious training and spent most of my life as an unbeliever, never bothering to find out what it was I didn't believe in. I was married in New York in a Park Avenue church because it was the socially acceptable thing to do, but from that day on it was to be many a year before my husband or I again saw the inside of a church. I had a wonderful husband, a graduate of the United States Naval Academy, who was later to become an executive of Gulf Oil Corporation. We had two beautiful children, and I became a successful free-lance magazine writer. Who needed or wanted God? Only the poor, the suffering, the weak, and we weren't any of these. And then I inadvertently attended a healing service. As a result of what seemed to be a purely haphazard accident, my life was to be forever changed.

To be sure, my first book had ended not as the exposé I had originally intended but as the story of my journey into faith. Nevertheless, I was a professional writer and this was just a book. True enough, I now believed in God, but at that time I certainly had no intention of devoting my entire life to Him. I was living a full and satisfying life, doing what I wanted to do and having fun doing it.

During the fall of 1956, when my first book was pub-

lished, I was invited to speak at the International Order
of St. Luke Conference, a religious conference in Philadelphia, which was attended by numerous clergymen. I received many requests to speak on the healing ministry
and began to accept them. As my children were young
and at home, I refused to leave them overnight, and
wherever I went I managed to fly home the same day on
which I spoke. There was one exception to this: I received
and accepted an invitation to lead a three-day mission
at an Episcopal church in a far-distant state.

At that time I had no idea what a "mission" was; all I
knew was that I was to give three addresses on successive
nights. When I arrived I was informed that each evening
address was to be followed by a healing service at which
I was to administer the laying on of hands with the participating clergy. I demurred strongly, never before having
laid on hands or prayed for the sick. However, my pro-
tests were in vain, and in fear and trembling, I did what
I was told.

The rector of the church was a firm believer in the
healing ministry, but his new assistant did not share
his sentiments. The young priest made abundantly clear
his disapproval of both the ministry of healing and of me,
a woman, performing a sacramental rite.

At the end of the second healing service the rector
knelt in moving humility to receive the laying on of
hands from me. Under the circumstances, the assistant
rector could hardly fail to follow suit. As I laid hands
on him, there was a loud crack, almost like a bomb
exploding. I jumped, having no idea what had happened.
Fifteen minutes later the mystery was solved: The crack
had been the sound of a long-dislocated bone in the young
man's body snapping back into place. It need hardly be
added that the young assistant became at that moment
one of the great champions of the healing ministry, and

from that time on, I became increasingly involved in the ministry.

As I realized what was happening to my life, I fought, I kicked, I ran; but surely and relentlessly God pursued me. He caught and held me fast in the net of His love. Holding me there enmeshed, He transformed my life by His touch. He drove me to my knees not by force but by love. And by His love He has kept me there, no longer struggling, but now in complete happiness and joy.

I was to learn over the years that it is by love that God works. Love is His power to convert and change lives, His power to heal and to mend all brokenness. His love enables us to say, "I will not be offended in Him" (Matt. 26:33) no matter what happens, and His love calls us to obedience and makes it our joy to obey, no matter how rough the road or difficult the way.

I was to learn, as I had never even remotely conceived before, the fullness of the truth that God's grace is indeed sufficient, and that His strength is made perfect in weakness.

I was to learn that His grace and His strength never fail, and that with Him all things are indeed possible. And I was to have reaffirmed for all time the greatest of all His promises: "Lo, I am with you always, even unto the end of the world" (Matt. 28:20).

Chapter 2

TOUCH AND GO: CONVICTION CONFIRMED

I REMEMBER WELL a woman in the terminal stage of cancer who flew to a healing service at Calvary accompanied by her nurse. I had agreed to speak with her for a few minutes before the service, and as she walked into the room the light of Christ emanated from her entire being. Her body was feeble and wracked with cancer, but she was filled with the joy of the Lord.

As she told me something of her condition, I asked her if she was afraid to die.

"Oh, no," she replied. "Actually I long to be wholly with Christ. However, as life is a gift of God, I felt I must do all possible to preserve it, lest there is more He wants me to do here. This is why I felt I had to come to Pittsburgh to attend this particular healing service."

In these words I heard the true Christian answer, and I knew this woman to be whole in Christ, regardless of the state of her body—and whether she lived or died.

After years of counseling and observation as well as experiential knowledge it is my firm conviction that one cannot live a true Christian life without having a Christian philosophy of death. That is, one cannot fully live the life abundant our Lord came to bring us (John 10:10) until we are unafraid to die, until we realize that at this very moment you and I are living in the midst of eternal life.

Death for the believer is not nihilism; it is the fullness of life in Christ. The early Christians lived with spiritual power and met death with joy because they knew this truth. The average Christian today either refuses to think of death at all, or his entire life is diminished because it is colored by what amounts to a psychopathic fear of death. It has long seemed to me that the problem of the Christian should not be his fear of death, but rather the dilemma expressed by Saint Paul when he said, "For me to live is Christ, and to die is gain. I am in a strait betwixt the two" (Phil. 1: 21, 23). Yet whenever I have spoken of death as the final triumph for the Christian, and not the ultimate disaster, a number of people have invariably said to me, "You can talk this way now—but just wait until you are faced with death, and you'll be as frightened of it as I am."

For a long time I had no answer to this, but now I have, for on a Tuesday evening several years ago, on my way to lead a mission in another state, I was faced with death. I was scheduled to make a connecting flight to my ultimate destination, but the connecting plane experienced mechanical trouble, and at five o'clock, after waiting in the airport for four hours, word came that this plane could not be repaired, and the next flight out would be the next morning.

It was imperative that I reach my destination that night. After much inquiring I discovered that an air-taxi service operated between where I was and where I was going. The next such flight was scheduled to leave at seven o'clock, so after telephoning the pastor of the mission church to say my plane was scheduled to arrive at 7:45, I took up my vigil at the air-taxi counter.

At last seven o'clock came, and I heard the welcome words, "Here comes the pilot now. As you're the only passenger, he'll take you in the two-seater."

I looked up, and could see no one coming except a middle-aged man in blue jeans and a torn sweater. This, it turned out, was the pilot.

He took my bags and led me to a tiny plane. There was no ramp, no steps, and when I asked, "How do you get in?" he replied, "You climb up on the wing and crawl in."

It had started to rain—a slight drizzle—and I shuddered to think of the state of my pale beige fur coat after crawling along the dirty, wet wing. But I clambered aboard, grateful for any transportation, and sat in the seat next to the pilot. The cabin was pitch-black except for the dim glow of the instrument panel in front of us.

About ten minutes after take-off, we ran into a severe storm. There was a deluge of rain, and great flashes of lightning seemed to split the sky in two. The small plane hurtled about like a piece of paper in a hurricane.

Time went on and on. It seemed to me that surely more than the forty-five-minute flight time had elapsed, but I could not see my watch in the darkness. It got colder and colder inside the plane, until my teeth were actually chattering. The pilot spoke briefly into the radio mouthpiece, but I was unable to hear what he said above the ear-splitting noise of the engine. He then took out of his pocket what appeared to be a map, and asked me to hold a flashlight while he studied it.

The plane took a sudden plunge, and just as suddenly, I knew that something was badly wrong. I yelled at the top of my lungs to be heard above the engine: "Is something wrong?" By a scarcely perceptible shrug of his shoulders, I knew that the pilot had heard my question—and I also knew that he would not answer for fear of frightening me.

As the lightning and the plunging of the plane grew worse, I yelled again, "Please, I'm not afraid"—and the wonder of it was, I was telling the truth—"but I want to know. We *are* in trouble, aren't we?"

This time the pilot turned toward me and nodded. Then he did a kind and lovely thing: He reached out with his right hand and took my left, and squeezed it. By this compassionate gesture, I knew in just what serious trouble we were.

"I'm going to try to land," he said. "We can't possibly make it any further."

I could feel the plane descend. Rushing down in the blackness of the night, a small light seemed to leap forward to meet us. It was a light from a house. Far off in the distance to our right appeared the runway we were trying to make.

The plane ascended again, and the pilot said, "I'll have to make another try for it."

It was then that I realized that the radio was out. We had no communication with the airport, and visibility was zero. There was no radar to assist us, and at this point I realized that our chances of landing safely were virtually nil. I knew that I faced death.

Thoughts of my children flashed through my mind, and I wondered who would tell them. Then I prayed for the pilot, made a quick act of contrition, and with my hand in the hand of Christ—so close was He—I suddenly felt the greatest joy I have ever experienced. Wherever I was going, it was not into the unknown. Crystal clear I heard the words: "Today shalt thou be with me in paradise" (Luke 23:43).

What more does a Christian really need to know? Having long prayed that I might burn out and not rust out in

His service, I now felt an overwhelming gratitude for answered prayer.

"Into Thy hands, O God, I commend our spirits—that of the pilot and mine," I said aloud. And then, my voice drowned out by the roar of the engine, I sang lustily the Nunc Dimittis: "Lord, now lettest thou thy servant depart in peace, according to thy word. For mine eyes have seen thy salvation, which thou hast prepared before the face of all people; To be a light to lighten the Gentiles, and to be the glory of thy people Israel" (Luke 2:29–32). As I sang "Glory be to the Father and to the Son and to the Holy Ghost," I felt a tremendous jarring. My back seemed broken and my body strained so hard against the seat belt it seemed it must be cut in two. Then I felt the eerie sensation of standing on my head. Opening my eyes, I saw that we were nose-down in a field about two hundred yards from the runway. The pilot grabbed me, dragged me out of the plane, and told me to run in case of fire. As we ran over the rough field, stumbling and almost falling, three men ran out from the tiny airport building to meet us. "My God!" one cried, "We thought you'd gone down for sure!"

The pilot looked at me, took both my hands in his, and replied, "We ran into a bit of a storm, and had a little navigation trouble. With the radio out, I was flying completely blind."

I looked now at my watch. It was just after ten-thirty. We had been up in the air for over three and one-half hours.

By now storm warnings were out, and all planes were grounded. One of the men at the airport offered to take me in his car to my destination, a two-hour drive away. Before leaving, I called the pastor, who had been waiting for me for three hours. At eight-thirty he had been told that there was no word from my plane, which was apparently lost. At nine they closed the airport, and the pastor and his wife sat just outside the shut door near a telephone booth in case I should call. They had been in prayer the entire time they were waiting and had planned to remain there until midnight. If by then they had heard nothing, they were prepared to call my bishop in Pittsburgh and ask him to notify the children.

Meanwhile, the pilot and I, who had been through this experience together, had become the closest of friends, although we did not even know one another's name. We threw our arms around each other before we separated, and his parting words were: "I'm so sorry about this. It was the closest call I've ever had." Then, as an afterthought, he added, "Hey—how come you weren't scared?"

All I could think of to say was, "Because by the grace of God I am a Christian."

"Me, too," he said.

As I walked out of the little building, I said to him, "Be careful—and God bless and keep you."

He replied, "God was awfully close tonight, wasn't He?" I just nodded and stepped into the waiting car.

Now in the telling of this story and my own reaction to what I believed was impending death, I do not mean to imply that I don't love life. I do—and so should all Christians. But I also believe that all Christians should look forward to death with the joy of Saint Paul, knowing as he did that death is only another dimension of eternal life, and that in death lies that perfect wholeness which alone can be found in the fullness of Christ.

The mission that I had so nearly missed was marvelously blessed. The people's hope, expectancy, and hunger for God were vividly apparent—and He honored those elements with an almost incredibly abundant outpouring of the Holy Spirit.

There were healings of every kind: of fear and anxiety and depression, of broken relationships, of grief, and of course there were numerous physical healings. These included the instantaneous disappearance of a large abdominal tumor, the restoration of vision to one long blind, and the disappearance of symptoms of advanced Parkinson's disease (the woman wrote me a letter several weeks later, the first letter she had been able to write in fifteen years because of the tremor of her hands).

The case of a woman healed of crippling arthritis was particularly interesting. She had come to me the first day of the mission, bent double, walking with great difficulty with the aid of two canes. She was a woman of great faith, and at the end of our talk, I said, "In the name of Jesus, walk." Her back straightened, she handed me her canes, arose from her chair, and walked three times around the room. At first her steps were hesitant, then firm and sure. She came to all of the services, where she offered thanksgiving and prayed for others. Like the woman during our Lord's earthly ministry, she was permanently loosed from her infirmity (Luke 13: 10–17).

Then there were multitudinous healings of ruptured discs and spinal ailments of various kinds. Curiously enough, these are a frequent occurrence at healing services ever since the original injury to my own spine. I have never before witnessed so many healings of spinal trouble as over the past six years.

The healing of a little girl of about eight, of a minor affliction—warts—was one of the healings for which I was most grateful.

In the opening address of the mission, I had told of inadvertently attending my first healing service years before, when a little boy was healed of his warts. (Actually this healing had not impressed me at the time, knowing as I did that warts spontaneously disappear.)

On the second evening of the mission the little girl whispered to her mother, "Mrs. Neal says that God cares about my warts and will take them away, so I'm going

up to receive the laying on of hands." Up she trotted
with the glorious faith of a little child, and God did indeed take away her warts. To me healings of this kind are
as wonderful as the healing of any cancer. They demon-
strate so beautifully that to God nothing that concerns
His children is unimportant or unworthy of His healing
love, and that He is beyond all doubt a personal God,
who knows the number of hairs on each of our heads and
is aware of each sparrow which falls to the ground (Matt.
10:29, 30).

When I learned of the healing of this child, I remembered a small boy in Pittsburgh for whom we have long
prayed, but who has not as yet been physically healed.
Tommy, deaf in one ear, is the son of an Episcopal priest
of great faith in the healing Christ. He laid hands on his
son regularly, for a long, long time, completely convinced that his hearing would be restored. "Finally," he
says, "I realized that Tommy was not going to be physically healed—at least not right now. So I changed my
prayer to: 'God, if he can't hear me, let him hear You.'"
The prayer of this father was answered. Tommy is extraordinarily close to God, and who among us would
dare to say that this child is not whole?

Twisting to get in and out of the plane, plus the extremely rough landing, had badly injured my back again,
and the effects of the accident would be with me for
years to come. But I was so overwhelmed by the power
of God manifested during this mission that my own injury seemed completely insignificant. When the final
service was over and the people had gone home, the
participating clergy, as overjoyed and exhilarated as myself, were talking together in the sacristy as they devested.
I slipped away unnoticed and knelt at the altar rail of
the now darkened and empty church, thanking God for
the awesome power of the Holy Spirit which had been
so evident during the past three days. Offering Him once

more my injured back to be used for His glory, I prayed with all my heart that if because of my pain I were to be a more open channel for His healing grace, He permit me to keep it.

I was to think often of this prayer in the months to come, as the power of the Spirit seemed greater than ever before. I was fully aware of that narrow line between a neurotic desire to suffer, which then makes us impervious to the healing power of the resurrected Christ, and offering to Him the suffering we have, at the same time praying that His perfect will for wholeness be fulfilled in us. In the end I was satisfied that I was on the right side of the line. Hating pain of itself, I was not rejoicing in my infirmity because I then had more to offer God. I could not embrace the pain as pain—but I could embrace it as the cross by which I could share in Christ's death, and thus inevitably in His Resurrection.

If for reasons I did not understand God was using this pain as I knew He was—perhaps to purge and cleanse that I might be an increasingly open channel; perhaps to protect me from spiritual pride in order that I might be a better instrument—then I would not only gladly endure, but "glory in my infirmity that the power of Christ might rest upon me" (II Cor. 12:9). For the reason for my being was that He might be glorified and manifested through me.

This is not to say that in the pain-filled years ahead I did not falter. I did. It is not to say that I was never discouraged or at times demoralized by pain. I was. It is merely to say that in His mercy I never felt forsaken.

Chapter 3

LEAVE THE METHOD TO GOD

SOME TIME AGO, a young minister telephoned me long distance to ask prayer for his ill wife. During the course of our conversation, he remarked, "If my wife is healed, she will make a powerful witness. God will *really* be glorified in my church. This is why I'm so certain that she *must* be healed."

As I heard these words, my heart sank. Time and time again I have heard this rationale for healing expressed, and almost invariably the individual who is to *"really glorify God"* through his healing witness fails to recover. Why should this be? Surely it appears a worthy motive to desire healing so the kingdom may be advanced. I have spent many hours pondering this question and the seeming paradox involved. Gradually I have come to conclude that it is not the avowed motive but the attitude behind it which is at fault.

In our knowledge of the healing Christ and our subsequent enthusiasm for the healing ministry, we are often led astray by the false assumption that God can be glori-

fied only by a witness of physical healing. The truth is
that some of the most effective Christian witnesses I know
are those who are lying flat on their backs expectantly
awaiting their healing by God's grace and at the same
time are offering their suffering to be used for His glory.
I have seen the light of Christ shine with blinding
radiance in the eyes of those who are suffering in His
name and for His sake.

Those who are enabled by grace (for no one can do it
on his own) to suffer redemptively are far more whole
than the individual who may enjoy perfect physical
health yet is spiritually dead.

It is not difficult to glorify God when one receives
physical healing. It is when one suffers yet never loses
his faith in the healing Christ, when one offers his life to
God, confident that in His own way and time He will
bestow His gift of healing, that Christ can be glorified—
sometimes even more effectively than if an instantaneous
physical healing were to occur.

If my heart sank at the young minister's stated reason
for his assurance that his wife would be healed by the
power of God, it plunged at his next words: "Of course,
Betty can be cured by simple surgery, but she will make
a better witness if God heals her without medical
intervention."

Entirely unwittingly this young clergyman, as so many
others with this same attitude, was, in my opinion, guilty
of the sin of presumption. As God does not tolerate a lack
of humility, so He does not tolerate its twin, presumption.
To tell God how He must heal, to demand that He heal in
only one way, namely by the direct intervention of His
Holy Spirit, is surely an act of presumptive arrogance
on our part.

All knowledge is of God, given and revealed to men by
Him—and medicine is part of this knowledge. To reject it
is to reject a gift of God. The purpose of the healing

ministry is not to eradicate medicine, but to seek that cooperation of medicine and religion which will best assure the total wholeness of the individual.

Most certainly we pray for healing, but the means must be left to God. Sometimes He uses physicians, sometimes He heals without. Sometimes He uses surgeons, sometimes He Himself is the surgeon. I think particularly of a woman with a breast tumor. The morning following healing prayer the tumor had not only disappeared, but a thin, white scar, perfectly healed, was clearly visible. However, in the prayer that had been offered for this woman, we did not presume to tell God how to heal her. She had been scheduled for surgery within the week, and we had offered thanksgiving that God had revealed to man the means of skillful surgery, and that it was available to those who needed it. We prayed for the guidance of the surgeon, asking that the Great Physician heal according to His will. In this case, as in many, it was His will to heal by the direct intervention of the Holy Spirit.

Properly practiced, the healing ministry works in cooperation with the medical profession; it never seeks to supplant it. As physicians learn that we do not advocate that the sick stop their medication or discard their crutches, the original skepticism and hostility toward this ministry by the medical profession is being replaced by the endorsement of a growing number of doctors. Many of these who have seen medically inexplicable healings in their practice are now willing to attribute such healings to the power of God released by prayer.

In those instances where God chooses to heal through physicians, healing prayer gives strength and courage to the patient, and almost invariably he makes an unusually rapid recovery. A typical example is the case of a woman who recently underwent a mastectomy. Apprehensive and fearful, she attended a healing service the evening before she entered the hospital. As a result, she went to surgery

unafraid and in great peace. She made an extraordinarily
rapid recovery, suffering virtually no pain whatsoever
and refusing sedation. This kind of rapid and uneventful
recovery of the dedicated Christian has been remarked
by many physicians, including Dr. Graham Clark, eye
surgeon at Columbia Presbyterian Medical Center in
New York.

Healing prayer results in a divine quickening of the
entire healing process—a quickening which can be rather
mundanely likened to the baking of a potato in a micro-
wave oven, which takes just a few minutes, rather than
in an ordinary oven, which takes an hour. And not only
does the cooperation of medicine and religion result in
more rapid healing, but in more complete healing. Here
the spirit as well as the body is involved, and thus the
wholeness of the individual is assured—that wholeness of
the entire nature of man, which comprises body, mind,
and spirit.

Misconceptions of the healing ministry are many
and varied. Not long ago, for example, I received a letter
from a woman, obviously distraught, asking prayer for
her critically ill child. The woman knew nothing of the
healing ministry, but someone had given her my name,
and she had written in sheer desperation. She ended her
letter by saying, "A friend told me to take my daughter
to healing services, or at least for me to go on her behalf
as intercessor. This I refuse to do, as I don't believe in
forcing God."

In my reply I explained that the healing ministry is in
no way an attempt to coerce an unwilling God into healing. Instead, it is an attempt to permit His perfect will
for wholeness to be fulfilled in us. He proffers us His
healing because of His boundless mercy and love—not in
reluctant response to any efforts of ours to "force" Him
to heal. God cannot be forced. He does not coerce us,
nor will He be coerced by us. He heals out of pure com-

passion. This was one of our Lord's great revelations concerning the nature of God. Throughout His earthly ministry Jesus healed all who came to Him, thus revealing for all time the will of God in respect to disease and brokenness of every kind.

In the case of this medically incurable child, whose mother was to learn what the healing ministry really meant, God healed by the direct intervention of His Spirit.

Over the centuries countless lives have been lost because people have not believed or sought the healing power of the risen Christ. Conversely, many needlessly die today, because they eschew God's revealed knowledge, and insist that they be healed in a manner according to their wills, and not His.

In the recent past, an out-of-state couple flew to Pittsburgh to attend a healing service at Calvary. The woman had a large abdominal tumor, the man a double hernia. In the conference I had with them just prior to the service they told me that they had come to be made whole in Christ. This was a proper motive, and indeed the reason for the Calvary services. They had come, they assured me, filled with expectant faith. This was good, for expectancy is one of the laws of healing. Yet neither of them had consulted a physician since the original diagnosis had been made.

I explained to them that the healing ministry was not a substitute for medicine, that a healing service is not the equivalent of a visit to a doctor's office. I told them there should be close cooperation between medicine and the healing ministry. Nevertheless, frequently when physicians have given up all hope for a patient's recovery, the patient is healed by the power of God.

This couple had refused to return to their physician because, they said, their faith in God to heal made medical treatment unnecessary. This may have proved true in their case; it has been so in many others, but only when the patient leaves the method of healing in God's hands. The attitude of this couple disturbed me, for they were in a very real sense delivering an ultimatum to God: "He is going to heal us here and now—or else."

This is where the presumption comes in, that sin of the spirit which so often impedes the healing power of God. It is not that He ever intentionally withholds His healing, but any sin separates us from God, creating a divisive chasm across which His power cannot flow. It is not He who will not heal, but we who cannot receive that grace He stands always so ready to pour upon us.

It is a basic tenet of the faith that God works through men; and thus He works through doctors, even if the physician is not a Christian. God is the God of both atheist and believer. He exists whether or not we acknowledge Him, and not one of us on this earth could draw a single breath were it not for the Holy Spirit.

The couple to whom I attempted to explain all this had mixed reactions. The man understood what I was saying. The woman was angry—so angry that at the service she did not come up for the laying on of hands with prayer. Her husband did; he came not for himself, but for his wife, that she might understand what I had attempted to tell her.

This story had a happy and, it seems to me, extremely significant ending. The husband was himself completely healed by God, and his prayers for his wife were answered. She wrote me an apology for her attitude, telling me that she had reconsidered and gone to her physician. He had recommended surgery, and she wrote me several weeks after her operation. The tumor was benign, and her recovery was remarkably rapid. She stated in her letter: "I see now what you meant. I prayed for my surgeon and for my healing, and God healed me as surely through surgery as by the direct intervention of the Holy Spirit.

The hand of the Great Physician was on my surgeon's hand, and Jesus Himself stood with us in the operating room. I thank God for my doctors and for His healing grace made manifest in me."

A Pittsburgh woman attending the Calvary services offers a good example of one who committed an entire situation to God to do with according to His will. Her husband, a man in his forties, suffered from cataracts. He was under the care of an ophthalmologist who was awaiting the proper time to operate—which, the physician cautioned, would not be for a considerable length of time. Cataracts must reach a certain degree of "ripeness" before they are operable, and this ripeness occurs only when the patient is virtually blind. The waiting process is tedious and nerve-racking.

In addition to his frightening physical condition, this man was deeply worried about his work. He was a salesman on the road all week, necessarily driving his car wherever he went. As well as his wife, he had young children to support, and with encroaching blindness his job was in serious jeopardy. He was as concerned and anxious over the almost inevitable loss of his job as he was over the condition of his eyes.

The wife came to Calvary to intercede and receive the laying on of hands for her husband. Her first prayers were for the immediate healing of his eyes—and then suddenly a new thought came to her, surely inspired by the Holy Spirit. She changed her prayers to this effect: "Lord, I know that it is Your holy will that Bob be healed, and I know that You *will* heal him. But the *method* of Your healing I leave in Your hands. I pray therefore that Bob be either quickly healed—or that the cataracts will rapidly worsen to the point that the surgeon can operate. Whatever is Your will, I thank You for this healing."

The following Friday night when Bob came home for the weekend, he walked in the front door and said to his wife, "Sit down, honey, I have to tell you something." They sat down together on the sofa. As he put his arm around her, he said, "Now pull yourself together. I know that you've been praying for my healing, but God's answer is 'No.'" Bob paused for a moment and then delivered his blow: "I'm almost totally blind. It happened all of a sudden this afternoon, and I had to leave the car in Cleveland and fly home."

To Bob's utter amazement, his wife cried out ecstatically, "Thank God! My prayers were answered!"

At her husband's look of bewilderment, she explained. "Don't you understand? Now you can be operated on during your vacation, and you'll be as good as new when it's time to go back to work!"

That is precisely what happened. She drove her husband to the doctor next morning. The eye surgeon examined Bob, and surgery was scheduled for the following Tuesday morning. The operation was totally successful.

This is not to say that we are not confident that it is God's primary will that we be healed—but the timing and the method of the healing must be left to Him. This does not mean that we should not expect instantaneous healing. We should, for we should always expect the most, just so long as we do not attempt to dictate to God, and by our presumption thwart the working of the Holy Spirit.

God chose His own way to heal Bob. For reasons we do not know, He has chosen to heal others with the same affliction without surgery. Dr. C. B. King, an ophthalmologist in Canton, Ohio, reports, for example, that a patient came to him from another town for an eye examination. Dr. King found his eyes almost perfect. This man then told the physician that several years before, he had suffered cataracts in both eyes. Following the customary procedure, his ophthalmologist was awaiting the proper time for surgery. Meanwhile, as the patient's vision

worsened, his driver's license was revoked. This man then
began attending healing services, praying for healing in
God's own way. He was completely healed by the power
of God without surgery. Dr. King issued him a medical
certificate, and the man's driver's license was subse-
quently reinstated.

To demand that God heal in a particular way, according to our own desire, is to attempt to make of Him a
celestial lackey. We must ask Him for the fulfillment of
His holy will in us. We must place our confidence in Him,
knowing that He never makes a mistake; that whatever
way He choses to heal is the best way for us under our
circumstances and is in accordance with His plan for
us.

We go to Him in prayer; we come to His healing
church in order to be made whole in Him. At the same
time, we obey the admonishment to "honor the physician
with the honor due him," for "He gave skill to men that
He might be glorified in His marvelous works. There is a
time when success lies in the hands of physicians; for
they, too, will pray to the Lord" (Ecclus. 38:1, 6, 13
R.S.V.).

We should not, therefore, eschew the God-given
knowledge of men, but neither should we ever forget
the vital necessity of prayer so that we may be not only
physically healed but made spiritually whole. It is Christ
who integrates our total personality, and through Him we
receive healing on a far deeper level than medicine alone
can provide.

Chapter 4

"ALL SORTS AND CONDITIONS OF MEN"

NOT LONG AGO a self-avowed atheist categorically stated: "One has to be of a certain temperament, a particular emotional make-up, if one is to accept the Christian faith."

This statement is totally erroneous. First, Christ died for all men, and the gospel is equally applicable to everyone. Second, a mere glance at the history of the faith and some of its great leaders makes clear the extraordinarily wide diversity of temperament among Christians throughout the ages.

We see in Saint Peter, for example, a wavering, rather unstable personality; in Saint Paul, an unequivocating and authoritarian theologian. Later, we see the simple poet, Christ-like Saint Francis; the intellectual and self-willed Saint Augustine; the brilliant philosopher and theologian, Saint Thomas Aquinas; the illiterate French peasant, the Curé d'Ars, who could not pass his theological examinations and for years was refused permission by the church to hear confessions, but who became one

of the church's great priests to whom thousands flocked
from all over France, including some of the great digni-
taries of the church.

From the beginning of Christianity there have always
been disciples of markedly different temperaments and
talents, and so it is today. There is no one "Christian
temperament," and this is particularly evident in the
healing ministry, where we see all denominations com-
mingle. There is room in the faith for all backgrounds
and emotional make-ups, from the Pentecostals to the
most conservative Eastern Orthodox churches, from fac-
tory workers to business executives, from poets to scien-
tists. The one great bond is love, by which the Spirit of
God binds one to another.

We are all one in Christ, but fortunately we are not one
in our talents or intellects or emotional responses. Christianity is for all people for all time. Our Lord was not
crucified for "specialists," and each and every Christian
has something peculiarly his own to bring to Christ
and His body.

A woman with several small children once said to me,
"I feel swamped in a bog of trivia. I'm not doing anything worthwhile for Christ—just washing clothes and
getting meals."

I reminded her of Brother Lawrence (*The Practice of
the Presence of God*) and of how, amidst his pots and
pans, he glorified God. Nothing, no matter what it may
be, is "trivial" if it is done for the glory of God.

During His earthly ministry of healing, our Lord
ministered to people of every conceivable background.
He met each one's need by the appropriate method. Although the sacramental healing rite of the laying on of
hands is offered in obedience to our Lord's command,
"They shall lay hands on the sick and they shall recover"
(Mark 16:18), and although He himself used this
method (Luke 4:40, 41), He was not bound by it; He

healed in a number of different ways, as the situation and the personality warranted.

He healed frequently by touch, as in the case of the widow of Nain's son (Luke 7:11–15); by word, as with the centurion's servant (Luke 8:8). He healed by intercession (the Syrophoenician woman's daughter, Matt. 15:21–28); by anointing (the blind man, John 9:6). He healed through the forgiveness of sins, as in the case of the palsied man (Mark 2:3–12), and by exorcism, as with the dumb demoniac (Matt. 9:32, 33).

And so it is today: Particular illnesses, particular temperaments, may respond to different methods. Thus when people ask, "Must one receive the sacramental healing rites to be healed?" the answer is obviously "No."

Thousands have been healed by prayer alone, by petition and intercession. Many have been healed by simply reading about the power of God to heal, or by watching religious television programs, or by listening to radio evangelists. However, times without number, when we lay on hands in response to our Lord's specific command, people who have hitherto remained unhealed receive healing.

It is often and truly said that Christ commissioned His church to preach, to teach, and to heal. However, in respect to specific ministries of the church, I would alter these three imperatives to: "Preach the gospel, heal the sick, and do this in remembrance of Me." This is what our Lord said, and in this order. These words indicate to me three separate and distinct ministries.

Jesus did not say, "Preach the gospel, and as a result, the sick will be healed." While this sometimes happens, what He actually said was, "Preach the gospel *and* heal the sick" (Luke 9:2).

While I have often said that the sacrament of holy communion is the greatest of all healing services, and while many have indeed been healed through this sacrament, still one lays on hands out of obedience. The many members of religious communities who have been healed through the laying on of hands offer ample evidence that He meant what He said. These religious receive holy communion every day of their lives; they are recipients of remarkably powerful intercessory prayer when in need; yet many monastics have not been physically healed until they receive the specific healing rites.

At the other end of the spectrum are the non-sacramentalists who have been led to receive the sacramental rites and have received a miracle. I think in this regard of a woman almost totally incapacitated by a progressive crippling disease. Her husband is a minister in a non-liturgical church, and both to him and his wife any sacramental approach was anathema.

The sick woman had been prayed for for many months, apparently to no avail. It was during a healing mission that her husband sought me out. As his church is noted for its supposedly undeviating adherence to Scripture, I spoke to him of the scriptural authority for the laying on of hands; but his prejudice against the sacramental was too deeply ingrained to be quickly eradicated. However, he capitulated to the extent of taking one of my books home to his wife.

It was during the week following, which she had spent in studying the book, that she awoke suddenly in the middle of the night with the conviction that if she could receive the sacramental healing rite she would be healed. She awakened her husband and asked him to lay on hands.

He told me later, "I was in a state akin to panic. I didn't like the sacramental approach, and of course I had never in my life used it or that kind of healing prayer. But I saw how much it meant to her, so I went ahead."

As a result, his wife dramatically improved. The full use of her arms and hands has been restored, and she is able to take long walks, aided only by a cane, which she is certain she will soon be able to discard. She receives the laying on of hands regularly from her husband, who is no longer reluctant but eager to minister to her —and to his people—in this way. In her case, as in so many, the laying on of hands served as her point of contact with the healing Christ.

As there is also scriptural authority for unction (anointing with oil) for healing (James 5:14), many ask about the respective uses of these two rites. Although some churches use one or the other or both, personal observation leads me to believe that the laying on of hands is best used in public healing services, and unction reserved for private use in the sickroom. There are several reasons for this; among them is the fact that many who attend healing services come as intecessors, receiving the laying on of hands with special intention for another. This cannot be properly done with unction, which must be administered directly to the individual in need.

We can't fence God in, nor can we pigeonhole Jesus. God is not the private property of any one type of person or of any one branch of the church. The Holy Spirit works with power in evangelistic meetings and liturgical church services alike. The healing Christ will not be confined, and the ministry of healing is the great catalyst —not a *leveler*, but a *raiser*—where believing Christians are uniquely united by their faith in the healing Christ.

As the healing power of God is not restricted to any one church or method, neither is His response to prayer limited to any one form of supplication. This was beautifully illustrated during a recent mission. An extremely ill Episcopal priest was in attendance. After one of the services, he sent word that he wanted to see me. As we talked, it was clear that he was a strict Anglo-Catholic, and I realized that it was difficult for him to come to me, a woman, for help. I also realized how difficult it would be for him to receive a sacramental rite from a lay woman.

When it came time for the laying on of hands and healing prayer, I sensed intuitively that this very Catholic, older priest would feel more comfortable if some of his fellow-clergy were to participate. I asked him if he would like me to go back into the church and gather together any priests I could find. He nodded, so I did just this, managing to locate four.

We all laid hands on the sick man together, while I prayed the healing prayer. But it was not I who prayed, it was the Holy Spirit, Who knew far better than I how best to meet this man's need. I suddenly found myself on my knees and heard myself saying some of the great liturgical prayers that I didn't even realize I knew from memory. These were prayers which this priest loved and understood, and through them God worked to bless and heal.

The other priests joined with me as the prayers were concluded with the Sanctus from the Episcopal service of Holy Communion. Tears of peace and joy streamed down the sick man's face.

Immediately following this episode, a Pentecostal came to talk with me about his problem. Obviously his prayer-need could not be met with liturgical prayers from the Episcopal Book of Common Prayer. For him, the Holy Spirit prayed in me in an entirely different way, this time pleading the Blood of Jesus. This prayer the supplicant understood, and was blessed by God through it.

God meets the need wherever it is, and the Holy Spirit intercedes according to His will (Rom. 8:27). Thus the prayer-requirement, whatever the background or temperament of the supplicant, is met.

The diversity of temperament among all Christians emphasizes the dual nature of each believer: The Chris-

tian knows that joy which no man can take from him and
at the same time carries within himself a broken heart.
Our hearts break because we know that by our sins we
continue to break the heart of God. They break for the
world, and for all those who suffer. Yet as we seek to
fulfill the law of Christ by bearing one another's burdens
(Gal. 6:2), we are simultaneously filled with a curious
joy. It is as if our hearts, broken as they are by the world's
suffering, nonetheless serve as receptacles for the joy we
have in Christ—for we know that in Him all suffering is
overcome.

In the healing ministry we speak continually of claim-
ing the promises of Jesus. These promises do not apply to
only one kind of person; they are for all believers. "Ask,
and it shall be given you" (Matt. 7:7), our Lord said;
"And all things, whatsoever ye shall ask in prayer, believing, ye shall receive" (Matt. 21:22).

There is a condition implicit in these and all His promises; namely, that we must ask according to His will.
Everything we ask of God must be founded on His basic
premise and fundamental promise: "If ye abide in me,
and my words abide in you, ye shall ask what ye will,
and it shall be done unto you" (John 15:7).

So no matter what we ask of Him, it is a primary con-
dition that we abide in God and His words abide in us.
Only then can we say with the confidence of Jeremiah,
"Heal me, O Lord, and I shall be healed; save me, and
I shall be saved" (Jer. 17:14).

"If thou canst believe, all things are possible to him
that believeth" (Mark 9:23). We pray for that sort of
dynamic faith that enables us to *really* believe that all
things are possible with God. But as we pray, we must
watch our motivation: We must determine whether we
desire the gift of faith merely that we may receive what
we think we want, or whether we desire it so that we may
believe in Him Whom we ask.

I remember well a man suffering a veritable hell of

pain, who could not get his mind off the pain long enough to want in his heart anything but relief from his agony. His nurse, an unbeliever, looked askance when I spoke to him of the love of God, of how Jesus suffered for him, of how Christ looked upon him now with infinite compassion, suffering for and with him.

As I spoke, this man understood for just a fleeting second something of God's love; and for just a moment he wanted God Himself—the experiential knowledge that God did indeed abide in him. That moment was enough, and the pain left him.

To claim the promises of Jesus means to stand firm in our conviction that God does not lie, and that if we ask according to His will, it shall be given us. And we can know, with a knowledge of the spirit given by the Spirit, that "Eye hath not seen nor ear heard, neither have entered into the heart of man, the things which God hath prepared for them that love him" (I Cor. 2:9).

When we dare to claim His promises, marvelous things happen—but if they are to happen, we must be in His will. This is what He means when He says, "Verily I say unto you, whatsoever ye shall ask the Father in my name, He will give it to you" (John 16:23). To ask in His name is to request according to the will of God: otherwise we dare not ask. To know His will means to desist from asking, and to remain silent so that we may hear. It means to empty ourselves of self, so that we may be filled with His Holy Spirit. It means to stop champing at the bit of our own desires and learn to wait patiently, quietly, and confidently, until in peace He leads us to that door He wants us to walk through, the door that leads us to the next portion of the plan He has for the lives of each one of us. This is all we need to do, but of all things it is the most difficult, so anxious are we to manage and manipulate our own lives, making our own important decisions apart from God.

Here the line is close between a complete and vacant

passivity where we do nothing but coast aimlessly along, and a creative, active response in which we do indeed take action—but by God's, not our own, volition. For it is God and not ourselves in whom we live and move and have our being (Acts 17:28).

The promises He made were to His first disciples, who knew and loved Him well. Thus they were made to us, regardless of our church affiliation, our color, our background, or our temperament. He says to us as He said to those who followed Him two thousand years ago: "I am come a light into the world, that whosoever believeth on me, should not abide in darkness" (John 12: 47); "If any man serve me, let him follow me" (John 12:26).

As we are inheritors of the kingdom, but must claim it if we are to possess it, so, if we would claim His promises, must we believe in our heart His words when He says, "I am the way, the truth, and the life" (John 14:6). For without Him, we cannot find the way; we cannot know the truth; and we have no life.

Chapter 5

DELAYED HEALINGS

INSTANTANEOUS HEALINGS have increased greatly over the past few years, due most probably to the slowly but surely growing faith of the church. Nevertheless the majority of healings today are gradual.

This is in contradistinction to our Lord's earthly healing ministry, where all the healings recorded in Scripture were instantaneous; the only exception is the case of the blind man at Bethsaida (Mark 8:22–25).

Our Lord laid hands on him, and then asked if he could see. The man said, "I see men as trees, walking." Jesus immediately laid His hands again upon the man's eyes. When He removed them this time, the once-blind man was completely healed. He was now "restored and saw every man clearly."

During a recent mission I was privileged to witness a healing which was startling in its similarity to this gospel account. There was a young woman who worked nights and thus was unable to attend the mission's evening healing services. She asked, therefore, if she might bring her long-blind mother to the church next day to receive the laying on of hands with prayer. I agreed, and we arranged to meet in the rector's study after the morning session in the church. (In cases like this it is impossible to minister to one individual in the church during the day. The entire congregation seems possessed of a sixth

sense, and everyone present at the daytime sessions
wants to come up for the laying on of hands. This results in two healing services a day, which is an impossible
situation when there are hundreds on whom to lay
hands.)

Immediately after the morning service, I met with the
daughter and her mother as planned. After the blind
woman had received the healing rite, she said, "I can
see light." Then she seemed to focus her eyes on the cross
around my neck, and said in a hushed tone, "I see a great
concentration of light in the form of a cross."

The daughter, very excited, asked, "Mother, can
you see what color dress Mrs. Neal is wearing?"

The older woman shook her head. "It is pale," she
said, "but I can't tell the color."

The account of the blind man in Scripture flashed
through my mind. Following the example of Jesus, I
quickly laid my hands again upon the woman's eyes,
and I prayed. When I had finished, she looked straight at
me. Tears of joy streamed down her face as she said in
an awe-struck voice, "Now I can really see you, Mrs.
Neal. You have on a white dress and a silver cross is
around your neck." Her vision was completely restored.

This healing was delayed only a few moments. Why is
it that most healings are considerably more gradual?
Sometimes the reason is obvious. There may be blocks
within the individual, spiritual sins such as resentment
or hostility that impede the inflow of God's healing power.
When such factors do not appear to exist, we must suppose that the delay in healing is due to a weakness of
faith in the church as a whole. This was the belief and
the explanation of the ancient church when healings
failed to occur. Then there is the self-evident fact that
none of us is Jesus Christ, and hence we are not the completely open channels for healing that He was. Finally,
I am not convinced that there is not divine purpose in
many delayed healings.

I think often of some of the instant and extremely dramatic healings I have witnessed: the man long paralyzed who walked; the woman instantly healed of skin cancer; the man long deaf whose ears were opened. All failed to return to give thanks, and all of them promptly forgot or ignored the source of all healing. The spirits of these individuals were left untouched, and thus they were not healed in the way that matters most. They were not made whole, and it is wholeness we seek in the healing ministry. We consider the ten lepers, only one of whom returned to give thanks for his healing. It was to this one alone that our Lord said, "Thy faith hath made thee whole" (Luke 17:11–19).

While it is true that in many cases the healing of the spirit—the closer union with God, which is the primary purpose of the ministry of healing—*follows* a physical healing, in most cases the healing of the spirit comes first.

A typical example is the case of a woman suffering from a large ovarian tumor who attended a healing mission about a year ago. When she and I had a brief conference during the mission, I found her seething with jealousy, bitterness, and resentment. I explained to her that unless she was liberated from these destructive emotions, her chances of physical healing were slight indeed. Thus we made the burden of our prayer not the disappearance of her tumor by the intervention of the Holy Spirit, but the taking by Him of her spiritual sins which were hindering the inflow of His grace in her life. A wonderful thing happened to this woman, as it has to so many others. She told me later that after the healing prayer that evening at the service, the power of God came down upon her so mightily that it went through her body like an electric current and continued to do so throughout the night. A letter from her not long ago related that since the last night of the mission she had lost all her resentment, that she has been steadily growing in the knowledge and love of God; and since that time, her tumor has shrunk slowly but surely, until a recent medical examination proved it to be nonexistent.

Roots and pieces of what had been the growth were gradually eliminated by her system over a period of seven or eight months. All during these months this woman had engaged in a spiritual struggle. Because she had been highly expectant of instant healing, regardless of what I had said about the necessity of being rid of her own spiritual impediments, the fact that the power of God had flowed so strongly through her body that night of the mission had led her to think I had been mistaken— that she was indeed going to receive the instantaneous healing she sought. She reasoned that she would take care of the hatreds and resentments with which she was filled *after* her physical healing. But it didn't work that way. God's power going through her body was the seal of His promise that she would be healed when she met the requirements. I can only believe that it was God's purpose that her physical healing be delayed, so that when it came, she would be in every way whole.

In my own case, while I have been quickly healed of many ailments, the healing of my back has been torturously slow—but I believe that not one second of suffering has been wasted. This suffering was not the primary will of God, nor did He send it—of this I am certain. But I am equally certain that He has used my suffering for His glory and for His own holy purpose.

While we await the completion of a gradual healing, no suffering need ever be fruitless or unavailing. For while it is true that we believe that disease is not of the kingdom of God, we also know that when it is offered to Him it becomes His, and thus He sanctifies both it and the sufferer. Further, in a way we cannot pretend to understand but neither can we doubt, He will use our suffering on behalf of others if we will only ask Him. This is a powerful faucet of intercession given us by God, and obviously recognized by Saint Francis de Sales, who stated that whenever he was in dire need of prayer he invariably called upon someone who was in pain.

It has long seemed to me that redemptive suffering is one of the most awe-inspiring of all God's miracles. The trouble is that it is so rare. But those who know the healing Christ, those who with the Christian's sure and certain hope await their healing, can at the same time suffer redemptively.

There is nothing either morbid or contradictory in the healing ministry if, when you are suffering in any way, you pray that God will enable you to accept your suffering gladly, uniting it with our Lord's own perfect sacrifice. If we suffer in union with Him we have the inestimable privilege of sharing in a special way in the whole redemptive process. There can be a unique joy in offering our suffering on behalf of someone else who is in need of prayer. We have our scriptural authority for this in Saint Paul's words: "It is now my happiness to suffer for you. This is my way of helping to complete, in my poor human flesh, the full tale of Christ's afflictions still to be endured, for the sake of his body which is the church" (Col. 1:24 N.E.B.).

This is not to say that your suffering or mine has any *atoning* merit, for the Atonement belongs to Christ alone. He made the one full, perfect, and sufficient sacrifice for the sins of the world. No one of us can add to that. However, our suffering *does* lead to the setting free of life to be imparted to others. The words "for the sake of his body which is the church" mean that there is no separation between helping Christ and helping the church—for union with Him means union with all those who are in Him.

Here we come to a great paradox: Accepting your suffering never means that you must not simultaneously seek to resist and overcome it in His name. Although God does not send disease and suffering, He permits it. Victory over it becomes a challenge to our courage and our trust in Him. It is the test by fire, a test not willfully given by God but abundantly blessed by Him when it is successfully met. It is then that we hear in our hearts His words, "In thee I am well pleased," and we know a great joy, because by His grace, we have kept the faith.

The paradox involved here can by reconciled only by the Holy Spirit. It is He who teaches us through Scripture and revelation that suffering from disease is an evil, and that no man may desire it for its own sake. And yet in offering it to God to be used on behalf of another it is redeemed and thus becomes creative and constructive.

How do you offer your suffering? By praying something like this: "Lord, I offer you my sins, my contrite heart, my suffering, my entire life, such as it is—to be used for Your glory—and please use it on behalf of John, whose need is so great." If you so pray with your heart, He will use your offering as you ask.

I remember well the young woman who came to Calvary for the first time in a wheelchair, her face white and drawn, her body racked by the pain of cancer which no drugs could alleviate. On that particular night I happened to speak of offering one's suffering on behalf of another. The following week the young woman was back again, this time her face radiant. She told me that she had "practiced" all the preceding week the things I had suggested. Not only was the friend for whom she offered her pain healed, but she herself had dramatically improved. "The thought that my suffering was not wasted," she said, "but used by God to help someone else, has made the difference. This knowledge is better than a shot of morphine in so far as making one's own pain endurable."

What happened in the case of this young woman happens to many persons. We offer our suffering in union with His, and not only are those for whom we pray helped but, unsought and unasked, our own pain is very frequently relieved. How this "works" is one of God's greatest mysteries—but that it does work in many cases is beyond any doubt.

We learn from the Cross that all life is to be vicarious. Christ's sacrifice was for us a vicarious sacrifice; that is, He suffered in our stead. The offering of our suffering on behalf of another is, in a sense, God's vicarious sacrifice in continuing action, in which we have the great privilege of participating in an infinitesimal way, holding always before us this promise: "If we suffer we shall also reign with Him" (II Tim. 2:12).

During a group discussion a woman asserted rather belligerently, "The belief that suffering can be redemptive is man-made. There is nothing in Scripture to substantiate this idea."

In reply, I quoted to her: "Forasmuch then as Christ hath suffered in the flesh, arm yourselves likewise with the same mind: Rejoice, inasmuch as ye are partakers of Christ's sufferings" (I Pet. 4:1, 13).

Someone else in the group promptly retorted, "Then if we want to be really close to Christ, we should all seek pain."

No. To seek suffering in order to become more at one with Christ would be a prideful indulgence. One of the great saints of centuries ago who cruelly mortified his body confessed before he died that he believed he had been mistaken so to do, that he should have cared for, not virtually destroyed, his God-given body, the temple of the Holy Spirit.

There is a great difference between deliberately afflicting our bodies so that we may have more to offer God and constructively using the affliction we have while expectantly awaiting our healing which is His perfect will. It is said of Saint Teresa that during one period of her life she suffered from an ailment which made walking difficult, and yet she persisted each day in walking around the convent's spacious grounds. When asked why she did this, she replied, "I offer the pain to

God, praying that He will use it to lessen the weariness of a missionary I know."

The saint was actually enacting the words of Paul: "It is now my happiness to suffer for you. This is my way of helping to complete, in my poor human flesh, the full tale of Christ's afflictions still to be endured, for the sake of his body which is the church" (Col. 1:24 N.E.B.).

Throughout the day, when you offer your suffering to God on behalf of another in need, give thanks that He is using you as an instrument in imparting His life to His own household, the church. Then await with confidence the fullness of His healing power in your own life.

When night comes, remember these words of Saint Paul: "Never get tired of staying awake to pray for all the saints" (Eph. 6:18 Jer.). If you are sleepless for any reason, this is good advice not difficult to follow, and your very sleeplessness becomes one more thing you may gratefully offer. The curse of sleeplessness becomes a blessing if you use the long, still hours of the night not in cloying self-pity or restless tossing but in prayer on behalf of others who lie awake. As you offer your sleeplessness "for all the saints," you can be assured, although you do not know precisely how or why, that your intercessions will have great power, bringing comfort and solace to people you may not even know. And once again, unsought and unasked, will come to *you* a blessing. You will relax, cease twisting and turning, and lie quiet in His near presence. As you pray you will find great joy in the knowledge that you are somehow mysteriously mitigating the world's common suffering, as by sharing Christ's suffering you also share in His glory and thus become His true co-heir (Rom. 8:17).

"Such knowledge is too wonderful for me" (Ps. 139:6) will be your final thought. Committing your spirit and all those for whom you pray into His hands, you fall asleep.

Chapter 6

NOT MY WILL
BUT THINE

NOT LONG AGO I had a personal experience which simultaneously reinforced my conclusions and shed new light on why so many who sincerely claim that they desire healing so that they may better serve and witness to God's glory remain unhealed. At the same time I learned an invaluable lesson concerning unwitting presumption. Perhaps the reason this lesson had to be learned was that we who believe in the healing Christ are so unequivocally convinced that it is His perfect will that we be made whole that we are inclined to extend this certainty into areas where we cannot be equally sure of His will without a certain presumption.

The experience of which I speak had its beginning on a Monday night at Calvary, when in the healing-service meditation I spoke out strongly against the heresies so prevalent in the church today. I took for my text these words: "The Spirit speaketh expressly that in the latter times some shall depart from the faith, giving heed to seducing spirits, and doctrines of devils" (I Tim. 4:1). As

47

I spoke that night I was peculiarly conscious of a great blessing from God, a true anointing, so that it seemed to me it was not I who spoke but the Holy Spirit through my lips.

Filled with joy, I drove home after the service, thinking ahead to the mission I was scheduled to lead at the end of the week in another state. It was to be an extremely strenuous three days, and as I drove I thanked God that my back was now so much better.

The next morning, while dressing, I reached out to pick up an article on my dressing table, neither twisting nor bending in any way. As I picked the object up, I could hardly believe what happened: I felt that excruciating pain reminiscent of the airplane episode now five years in the past. This time it was even more severe. I gasped aloud the only prayer I could summon: "Christ have mercy."

I knew I should lie flat, but I was incapable of getting on my bed. Standing rigid, I called a friend and asked for prayer. I could not reach my physician, but my therapist agreed to take me at once. The immediate problem was how to get to his office. For no apparent reason I opened the nearby closet door. Looking up, I saw on the top shelf the long-forgotten cast in which I had been placed years before at the time of the original injury. With a prayer, I tentatively lifted my arms, managing to reach the cast. Laboriously I worked my way into it, and I called the custodian of my apartment, who drove me to the therapist.

Returning home after an agonizing trip to his office, I finally managed to get myself on the bed. There I lay, cast and all, for many hours.

Contemplating this freak "accident," there came a flash of recognition and I knew its source. I am well aware that many do not believe in Satan: I do, as surely as I believe in God. I recalled my meditation against heresy the preceding night and the blessing experienced from God; and I knew now that Satan had attacked again as he had so often in the past, and as he invariably does each time we come extremely close to God.

It is said that Satan is very clever, but my own experience leads me to think him abysmally stupid—for he never seems to learn that he cannot win. He can never reach those who love God through our bodies or in any other way, for in the end Christ is always triumphant.

I knew that day that there was a battle to be won, and engaged myself at that moment in the spiritual warfare of which Saint Paul speaks: "We wrestle not against flesh and blood, but against principalities, against powers, against the rulers of the darkness of this world" (Eph. 6:12). This is a challenge of which every Christian should be aware, and one from which he dares not shrink.

Reaching out for the cross on my bed table, clutching it so tightly that my palms bled, I said aloud, "In the name of Jesus I command you to leave me undisturbed." Knowing whom and what I was fighting, and in Whose name, gave me enormous strength.

At about midnight I struggled up to get a glass of water —a task that took me nearly an hour to accomplish. But it was the first step toward victory, for I was convinced that I could do all things through Christ. The remainder of the night I lay awake, in deep communion with God, and I was unafraid.

My great concern was the mission. It had been scheduled for over a year. I knew that in addition to the local people many were coming in from distant points. I simply could not disappoint all these people.

My attitude of prayer all that day and night had been, "Lord, I know it is Your will that I get to this mission. But I can't do it unless You get me on my feet. So please, Lord, raise me up."

The following morning I reached my physician, who hoped to inject the "pain points" with Novocain—but there were no "points." My entire back was involved. The only alternative seemed the hospital—I had been hospitalized before for far less—but hospitalization now was impossible because of the impending mission.

Later that day my rector brought me holy communion and anointed me. An hour later I felt curiously blessed, and so close to God I could not panic although I was still completely helpless and unable to move. Again and again I offered the pain to be used for His glory and on behalf of someone I knew who suffered. (This individual, incidentally, was healed of the pain of bursitis that same day.)

Saint Paul's words echoed and reechoed in my brain: "This is my way of helping to complete, in my poor human flesh, the full tale of Christ's afflictions still to be endured, for the sake of his body which is the church" (Col. 1:24 N.E.B.).

I began to feel a strange detachment from the pain, as if it were not my own but part of the world's pool of common suffering, a drop in the filling of the cup which in humility and with an inexplicable joy I could offer.

But it was now Wednesday night—perilously close to Friday morning, when I had to leave Pittsburgh. So again I prayed: "Lord, please raise me from this bed. You know I can't go anywhere in this condition."

Suddenly I received so strong an impression that it seemed as if I actually heard the words: "You are praying amiss." At that same instant I knew that the mission did not at all depend on my being there and that if I were unable to make it the pastor of the mission church would manage without me, for God would lead him to someone who would doubtless do a far better job than myself.

"When we know not how we should pray as we ought, the Holy Spirit maketh intercession for us—according to the will of God" (Rom. 8:26, 27); and so now did He pray in me: "Lord, I am not at all sure of Your will in this matter. You alone know best how You will be glorified. Forgive my presumption in believing that the mission would suffer if *I* were not there to witness to Your glory. Whether I am healed or not is entirely in Your hands. I have only one desire: that not my will but Thine be done in this whole matter."

As this prayer was concluded there was the momentary shining of a brilliant light, and I saw the shadowed outline of an outstretched hand. Instinctively I raised mine to meet it, and as I did so I heard in my heart these words: "I the Lord thy God will hold thy right hand, saying unto thee, Fear not; I will help thee" (Isa. 41:13).

A searing heat went through my body, and I broke out in so heavy a sweat that my bedclothes were soaked. I was still in severe pain and unable to get out of bed to change them. I lay motionless on the drenched sheet, but filled now with the assurance that I would be able to do the mission.

Next morning I got out of bed with a minimum of pain. I had my hair done, packed, took care of my always voluminous correspondence, and felt better with each passing hour. By Friday morning I was entirely well, and I left on schedule to lead one of the most arduous missions in which I have ever been privileged to participate.

It is God's perfect will that we be whole in every respect, body, mind, and spirit. Our Lord taught us by His earthly ministry the importance of physical healing. He also taught us that the curing of the body is not of primary importance; that our eternal destiny is not physical health, but holiness. "Ye shall be holy; for I am holy" (I Pet. 1:16). A prerequisite to holiness is the complete abandonment of our lives to Him. It is in this way that we are most likely to receive physical healing.

How often in the past have I urged people to pray the prayer of relinquishment, and how often in the past have I prayed it myself. Yet in the situation I have just described it took me two days to realize my failure. In my assumption that God must heal me then and there in order that I might properly serve Him on the mission, I was unwittingly guilty of the sin of presumption. I had fallen into the trap of believing that I knew better than He how to serve and witness to Him most effectively. The truth is, that however strongly we may feel that by our healing we may be better servants of Christ, it is He who is the sole judge. It is He and He alone who knows whether He wants us to serve or simply to be. I have at last learned beyond the shadow of any doubt that if He wants us to serve, He will enable us to do so no matter how great our weakness, for with God nothing is impossible. His grace is always sufficient for the fulfillment of His will.

I have learned how mistaken we can be in our zeal to serve. It is our devotion to Him, our willingness to be used *by* Him and not necessarily *for* Him, that He most wants.

"Can ye drink of the cup that I drink of?" He asks (Mark 10:38). Like James and John, we answer quickly and without hesitation: "We can." But we are to discover that it is far more difficult to drink of the cup than to serve, and far easier to serve than to be poured out.

The mission was spectacularly powerful. Rarely have I seen so tremendous an outpouring of the Holy Spirit, the risen Christ present in all His glory and power.

In the past I have often commented on what I choose to call the spiritual law of difficulty. This law seemed to be operative so consistently that I believed it could not be pure happenstance, but rather the working out of a true spiritual law. The events of the past six years have changed what was personal opinion into a firm certitude. The more difficult it is for an individual to attend a healing service, the greater the sacrificial effort and expenditure of time involved, the greater the blessing to the supplicant. If you are disabled or in pain, if you come to healing services at personal cost, God will abundantly bless you—for in your effort, in spite of sacrifice or obstacle, you have performed an act of faith which is pleasing in His sight. This is one of the reasons I urge the sick and suffering to come in person to the Calvary weekly services when at all possible if their physician permits.

The healing ministry is at once the most subjective of all the ministries of the church and one of the most powerful instruments of intercession God has placed in our hands. The intercessions do not go unheard or unhonored by God, and for those too incapacitated to attend in person, intercession is sufficient. Many and marvelous are the healings so wrought, but whenever an individual is able to come on his own behalf, he should do so. This signifies the act of faith God desires of you and for which He blesses you.

At the same time, the more difficult circumstances are for the one who ministers, the more power seems to be released. I have cited illustrations in the past concerning the operation of this law as it has applied to me [1]—for example, the traveling over treacherous, icy roads to a hospital at two o'clock in the morning to see a patient and the leading of missions under extreme discomfort. However, the increased outpouring of the Holy Spirit under the conditions I had previously reported pales before the power released during more recent years when I have worked under a severe physical handicap, a handicap increased by late planes, torturously long lay-overs in airports, and bad weather.

[1] Emily Gardiner Neal, *Where There's Smoke* (New York: Morehouse-Barlow, 1967), p. 55.

On one occasion, for instance, the car placed at my disposal stalled, and I was forced to walk over half a mile in a blizzard, with the temperature (taking into account the chill factor) at forty degrees below zero. On another occasion it was necessary to travel to and from the mission church over snow banks so high that the compact car carrying me would crawl laboriously to the top of each bank, then drop back to the road with a jar calculated to break every bone in a human body! And long shall I remember being stranded (fortunately I was returning from a mission) in a snowed-in airport, standing in line six hours to change my ticket, and finally being housed in an airport motel room. Here I remained in total isolation for thirty hours, cut off from the dining room or any room service by an ice storm of unprecedented severity. And I recall as well suffocating in Midwest heat, with the thermometer at 106 degrees, and no air conditioning!

When three such experiences in a row were followed by two forced plane landings in rapid succession, each resulting in further injury to my spine, a friend, perhaps understandably, said to me, "Don't you think these continual difficulties and out-of-the-ordinary hardships are evidence that God wills you to stop leading missions?"

My answer was "No." While it was perfectly obvious that the life I was living was scarcely conducive to physical healing, and while it was equally clear that if I stopped working I would be spared much physical pain, I knew with every fiber of my being that it was God's will that I continue. It was with this knowledge that I realized most forcibly how erroneous is the impression given by many of us who work in the healing ministry that physical suffering is something to be avoided under all circumstances.

While we believe that pain is not the will of God, nevertheless there are times when we cannot do His will without suffering. At such times there is no question of choice: The transcendent desire is obedience no matter what the cost. And it is a cost joyfully paid, for I have learned over the past years that there are far worse things than physical pain. I was compelled to go on; my compulsion was the love of Christ. Some spoke of courage, not realizing that my efforts took no courage whatsoever, for had I been disobedient to what I knew in my heart was the heavenly vision (Acts 26:19), the ensuing spiritual anguish would have been intolerable. Furthermore, my ability to continue was in no way due to my own willpower, as some have suggested. No willpower that I could have summoned would have been sufficient. It was only the imperative surrender of my own will, which led in turn to complete dependency on Christ in whom lies all strength, that made it possible for me to go on.

My conviction of God's will in the matter was an inner knowledge of the spirit, but one of the visible means for my certainty lay in the overwhelming power released during healing services when the going was especially hard. The reason for this seems clear: In great physical weakness one can do nothing on one's own. Thus He and He alone led these missions.

And so it was with the mission mentioned earlier. I knew it would be extraordinarily blessed: Not only had *I* such difficulty getting there, but the church was filled with the lame, the halt, and the blind, many of whom had endured an extremely long bus ride to get to the mission; all of these people had come at great sacrifice of time, and most of them at great cost in terms of physical pain.

The first healing was a dramatic one, of a type I have seen with great frequency over the past several years. I saw out of the corner of my eye a man walk up to the altar rail with a brisk and unfaltering stride. He knelt for the laying on of hands with prayer. As he walked back to his pew, he was limping so badly that two ushers rushed to his assistance. I have learned not to question God, but I remember thinking, "God does *indeed* move in mysterious ways"—for this man had walked to the altar rail in perfectly normal fashion, and he left it apparently crippled!

Later in the mission I learned what had happened. One of this man's legs had been two inches shorter than the other, so he was wearing a built-up shoe. At the altar rail, his shortened leg had lengthened two inches and was now equal with the other—hence the limp.

A young boy in a wheelchair, who had been paralyzed and without speech since an automobile accident several years before, regained considerable use of his limbs. In the middle of the service he stood up in his chair and spoke his first words since the accident: Loudly and clearly he proclaimed, "Praise the Lord!"

Then there was the child with leukemia, a clergyman's son. At the final healing service, as I prayed that the Blood of Jesus flow through the body of this child, I had the conviction that he was healed. Before leaving the church that night I asked the father to administer holy communion daily to his son, although the child was only four. This he agreed to do. Several years after the mission, the boy's disease has been, according to his physicians, "in an unexpectedly long state of remission." This period of remission has been unbroken since that final healing service. Coincidence? I think not, in view of similar long remissions of acute leukemia under similar circumstances.

Of four retarded children for whom healing prayer was offered, three have made continued progress toward normalcy. Physical healings during the mission were dramatic and numerous. Equally amazing was the healing of a young drug addict. For three days during the mission he took no narcotics whatsoever. Although on hard drugs, he suffered no withdrawal symptoms, and he lost all craving. A follow-up for some months indicated that the healing was permanent.

In the same category was an alcoholic, whose wife was threatening to leave him and take their children. During the mission this man lost all desire for alcohol. A year later he had not had, nor did he wish to have, a drink.

Throughout the mission the church was vibrant with the presence of God. People were responding to His love in ways they did not themselves comprehend. They were performing the most extraordinary acts of kindness one for another; one young man drove 220 miles round trip between the afternoon and evening services to bring a relative of someone at the mission to the final healing service.

People were experiencing the supernatural love of God in an unprecedented, and to them unfamiliar, way. I vividly recall a registered nurse who, blind for four years, regained her sight. At the coffee hour following the final service this woman, tears of joy streaming down her face, told me how she had felt *my* love for her pour through her as I laid on hands.

"How could you so love a total stranger?" she asked me.

Of course, it was actually not *my* love but the love of Christ she had experienced. *I* did not even know I had laid hands on her until she told me.

The love of Christ washed over everyone there, healing not only bodies and emotions and spirits, but broken relationships of every kind. Typical of these was a broken marriage. The couple, who had already parted, were induced by friends to come to the mission. They came separately, sitting in different sections of the church, and at the first healing service came up to receive the healing rite at different times. At the second healing service they found themselves, surely through the work of the Holy Spirit, unexpectedly kneeling at the altar rail side by

side. As prayers were offered that they might manifest
to each other the love of Christ, the healing actually
began. On the final night of the mission, they came to the
service together, and they arose from their knees transfigured. I was to receive a letter several months later
signed by both. It told me of their new-found happiness
together in Christ, to Whom they have committed their
lives. The Great Reconciler had done His work.

One of the healings for which I was most grateful was
that of a woman in her early forties. I had noticed her
each night being half-carried to the altar rail by
friends. At the end of the mission I learned her story—
not an uncommon one, but always wonderful to hear.
She was in the terminal stages of cancer, and her physician had given her only a few weeks to live. She came to
me at the conclusion of the final healing service, her face
radiant, and said, "Mrs. Neal, you simply can't imagine
my sheer terror of death. During this mission I have experienced the reality and the love of God. Now I no
longer fear death, but I look forward to being wholly
with my Lord with the same anticipation as a child on
Christmas morning."

Whether this woman lived or died I do not know. But
if she lived, she lives in Christ, and if she died, she died
in Him, experiencing her healing in His own way—
wherever and however He chose to heal.

That final healing service was indeed Christ triumphant. Every single person who came to the altar rail
came to offer praise and thanksgiving to almighty God.
Each and every one committed or recommitted his life
to Christ as his Saviour and Redeemer. And this, of course,
is what the healing ministry is all about, and this for me
determines the "success" of a mission. Marvelous as are
the physical healings, wonderful as are the healings in
every area of life, the greatest of all healings and the
greatest of all miracles is the conversion of the soul.

Chapter 7

HOLINESS AND WHOLENESS

DURING A RECENT MISSION an eighteen-year-old boy planning to enter the ministry asked me, "If someone were sufficiently holy, would he be sick?" At first glance this question may appear naïve, but in actuality it is extremely astute. Our subsequent discussion led into an area in which there is much confusion, an area too often left untouched by those of us in the healing ministry. As a result of this neglect, considerable unnecessary suffering is caused.

I explained to this young man that no one on earth is immune from illness, that as long as there is evil in the world, there will be suffering; and there will be evil on earth as long as man inhabits it.

Even as I spoke, I realized that too many people, lack ing an adequate understanding of the healing ministry, tend to equate holiness with physical wholeness.

It is true that the words "holiness" and "wholeness" have a common root. Most certainly it is God's primary will that all of us be physically as well as spiritually

whole; otherwise, over one-third of the gospel would not
be devoted to our Lord's earthly healing ministry. However, His perfect will is often circumvented by reasons beyond our individual control, such as the evil and unbelief of the world, of which we are all victims. That His
primary will is temporarily deflected does not mean that
an individual who happens to be physically ill cannot
be gloriously whole in Christ.

There are many people like a woman I know who in
her early forties is afflicted with a rare and devastating
type of arthritis. This disease causes progressive crippling
and unremitting, almost intolerable, pain. I was asked
to minister to this woman, now bedridden. As I entered
her room, there was no mistaking the radiance of Christ
that shone from her eyes. She expectantly awaits her physical healing, but in the larger and most important sense she
is even now whole in Christ. She dwells in Him, and He
in her. To enter her presence was for me a benediction,
as it is for all who know her.

The young man went on: "If holiness does not assure
one's physical well-being, why do you speak continually
of growing in grace and holiness, of the need to establish
a closer union with God, so that physical healing may
occur?"

The reason for my emphasis on this closer relationship
with God, which obviously must result in increasing
holiness, is this: The master key to all healing is found in
the words "Seek ye first the kingdom of God." As Christians we do not seek physical health for health's sake; we
are called to seek God for *His* sake, to seek Him above
all else and for Himself alone. It is only then that we can
reasonably expect that "all these things"—such as healing—"shall be added unto you" (Matt. 6:33).

The equation of holiness with physical health is un-
tenable and does a grave disservice to the sick. One of
the cruelest axioms I know, frequently quoted in the heal-

ing ministry, is; "There is no such thing as an incurable disease, only incurable persons." There is, to be sure, a half-truth here: There are indeed no incurable diseases in the sight of God. I have witnessed healings of virtually every disease known to man, many of them termed medically incurable. However, in the second part of this axiom, the clear—and mistaken—implication is that the *patient* is invariably responsible if healing fails to occur. This assumption is in direct opposition to the teaching of the ancient church, which did not ascribe such failure to the individual's lack of faith, but to the paucity of faith of the Body as a whole—which is to say, of the church.

Those who are suffering illness have enough with which to contend without adding an unjustifiable burden of guilt. It is a well-known fact that the sick frequently suffer from guilt feelings simply because they are sick. It is a peculiar psychological truth that non-Christians also harbor guilt feelings during an illness, possibly because they feel they are causing their families worry and expense. Perhaps the prevalence of guilt feelings during illness comes from the fact that buried deep in the unconscious of many individuals, Christian or not, is the erroneous idea promulgated by the church for so many centuries that God sends sickness as a punishment.

Christians who believe wholeheartedly in the healing Christ are prone to feel the guiltiest of all. Some of us who work in the healing ministry, including myself, must assume responsibility for at least part of the emotional suffering the believer too often endures. We state categorically—and correctly—that sickness is *not* the primary will of God. But there is danger in this teaching if we do not expand upon it. It is fatally easy for the sick to misunderstand, to wonder if, because they are ill, they are really in the will of God at all.

As one woman put it, "I have cancer, and I am seeking the healing power of God. However," she went on, "if His will is complete wholeness of body, mind, and spirit, does the fact that I am now physically sick mean that I am not in His will?" Then she added in a strained voice, "And suppose I am *not* healed here and now?"

This woman was a committed Christian. Her concern was not motivated by fear of continued physical pain, but rather by her extreme apprehension that if she were *not* healed it would mean she was outside the will of God.

For years I have observed this kind of apprehension among the sick who are dedicated to the healing Christ. It touched even an outstanding leader in the healing field who, stricken with a deadly disease, felt himself abandoned by God.

After extensive and intensive counseling among such individuals, during which I was able, I believe successfully, to allay their fears, I felt greatly blessed when I was injured—for my own suffering was not now compounded by feelings of guilt or confusion. Nevertheless, because of my personal experience I understand more clearly than ever before how such gross misapprehensions can occur. At the same time, I am now even more certain, because of empirical knowledge, that whether sick or well we are all safely held in the palm of God's hand, and He will never let us fall. I can say with complete assurance that you are most certainly in the center of His will if you are praying in faith for your total wholeness—for you are then praying according to His holy will.

If many Christians suffer needless guilt over their illnesses, there are likewise many who, as they await their healing, may be enduring great physical pain. Added to this there is frequently the mental anguish caused by the fallacious thought that they are somehow "letting God down" and proving themselves poor Christians if they acknowledge or dare to admit that they are suffering.

I have spoken earlier of the wonder of true redemptive suffering, and of how God can use your pain so that it becomes creative and productive. But pain of itself and for itself does not ennoble. It tends rather to demoralize, the patient becoming irritable and disagreeable. If sufficiently severe, pain can temporarily degrade the most spiritual among us to a purely animalistic level.

I know a wonderful Christian woman who is now extremely elderly and ill. Instead of possessing the tranquillity of old age, she is often cantankerous and querulous. She abhors this in herself, and constantly pleads for prayer that God may enable her in her suffering to be the sort of person He would want her to be. In truth she *is* that person: a devout and godly woman, whose spirit has been briefly trapped by her body.

Each individual has a different threshold of pain, some higher than others through no virtue of their own; some lower, through no personal fault. Those who are able to stand pain less well than others should feel neither guilty nor ashamed if they are making every effort to unite their suffering with Christ.

I remember that a long time ago, before I understood these things as I do now, how stupidly disillusioned I was when I witnessed the suffering of a great spiritual leader. I saw this man of God become against his will, though only for a short time, a demoralized wreck. In my ignorance I had the temerity to judge him. I did not comprehend then that the man I was watching was not, just for a little while, his true self. For the moment his pain had become a live and evil thing that simply appeared to my then-blind eyes to have taken him over. At the end, this saintly man died with a smile, the holy name of Jesus on his lips. Since then I have come to know that there can be intervals in the lives of the most courageous and godly people when pain seems to transcend all else. It only *seems* this way, for we are human as well as spiritual beings; and the suffering attacks our humanity, not our spirit, which is unscathed.

During our lifetime we all will suffer to a lesser or greater degree. You should feel no guilt if your cry "Lord, save" is involuntarily interrupted by the scream for physical help that seems to come from outside yourself: "Nurse—give me a hypodermic." Our Lord understands. Again we know the wonder of the Incarnation, for He has traversed the road of pain before us.

Before I was a Christian, one of the chief reasons for my agnosticism was the pain and suffering of all kinds I saw abounding in the world. Where was this merciful God of whom Christians were continually prating?

Finally I came to understand that it is not God but man who is responsible for war, for the hungry, for the deprived, for all social injustice. At long last I came to comprehend that one of God's greatest gifts to us is that of free will, but we have made of it a curse by its abuse.

"I have loved you, saith the Lord. Yet ye say, Wherein hast thou loved us?" (Mal. 1:2). One of the most compelling apologetics for the Christian faith so far as I am concerned has been my observation (and now my personal experience) that those who suffer most, in whatever areas of their lives, are usually the most aware of the love of God.

I think of a short time ago when after I had spoken in a church, one of the congregation came up to me, almost startlingly alight with the love of Christ. He then proceeded to tell me something of his life, and once again I marveled.

He had a twenty-year-old daughter who lay in an institution, as helpless as a six-month-old baby. His wife had committed suicide the year before. He had come to the church this night, seeking the healing power of God for his young son who suffered from leukemia. Surely, from a purely human viewpoint, this man had every reason to feel bitter and God-forsaken; yet the reverse was true. He spoke not in self-pity, but in gratitude for the love of God, which continually filled and upheld him. This the unbeliever cannot understand, but the Christian never doubts. He knows in his own life the truth of the words of French theologian Louis Evely: "When we suffer, the Father follows us with His eyes, with the same solicitude, the same admiration, the same anxious tenderness, the same wish to rescue and to help as when He looked on the Son as He went towards His Cross." [1]

Many of us do not fear death, but only the suffering we may have to endure in the process of dying. I vividly recall a woman who came to me directly after receiving her physician's verdict that her entire body was riddled with cancer. She said, "I know that Christ will heal me— if not here on earth, then when I am wholly with Him. The only thing I really fear is the suffering, for I know I don't bear pain well."

This woman suffered greatly, but I recall how often she received the laying on of hands with prayer, and how often her pain was either marvelously diminished or entirely eliminated for increasingly long periods of time. This is the mercy of God.

None of us understands the mystery of pain, suffering, and disease. Our Lord made no attempt to explain it. He simply healed, making crystal clear that it was not of the kingdom of God (Luke 13:16). He has given us the means of grace to combat the enemy: prayer, sacrament, and the healing rites. When we use these God-given means, we invariably receive from Him either surcease from pain or the strength to withstand it—and very often the gift of complete healing.

Although the fact that we are Christians does not mean that we shall not ever have to suffer, it *does* mean that with each respite from pain we as Christians can cry, "Save me, O Lord," and we shall be saved; we can cry, "Christ have mercy," and He will.

[1] Louis Evely, *We Dare to Say Our Father* (New York: Herder and Herder, 1965), p. 94.

The demoralization severe pain can cause is a transient thing. In the eyes of God it can and will be transcended by our inner knowledge, which never wavers, that Jesus is always with us. As we grasp His healing hand despite the pain, we are aware that we are safe within His providence, that in Him lies our healing if only we will hang on.

We know beyond the shadow of any doubt that in *everything* God works for good with those who love Him (Rom. 8:28 R.S.V.), and that nothing can ever separate us from His love. Though our lips may cry out in pain, our hearts are quiet in the serene knowledge that God will not let us suffer more than we are able to bear (I Cor. 10:13). Because our Lord suffered, He knows how we feel and why. He felt and endured all that we feel and endure, for He was like us in all ways, except that He was without sin (Heb. 4:15).

If, then, you suffer while you await your healing, if your body seems held in a vise of pain like an animal in a steel trap, don't feel ashamed or guilty if momentarily your desire for relief of pain seems to supersede your desire for God. Your body may be temporarily trapped, but your spirit will soar joyously free, made so by Christ. Remember always that *nothing* can wrest you from the His everlasting arms. In this knowledge lies His peace and joy, which He makes yours.

It is said that Pope John XXIII wondered whether he would suffer well when his time of tribulation came. By God's grace he endured magnificently, suffering in union with the Lord he loved. The words of one of his meditations when he lay dying [2] have been of inestimable comfort to me under many different circumstances. I have made them my own as I lay in pain; I have prayed them for my church, for my nation, for those who suffer, for all people everywhere. If you are suffering in any way;

[2] Pope John XXIII, *Prayers and Devotions* (New York: Doubleday & Co., Image Books, 1969), p. 328.

if you pray for others and for the world, perhaps you will find them a source of comfort and inspiration as have I.

> This bed is an altar; the altar requires a victim: I am ready. I offer my life for the Church, for the peace of the world and the union of all Christians. The secret of my priesthood is to be found in the Crucifix I placed before my bed. He looks at me and I speak to Him. In our long and frequent conversations at night, the thought of the redemption of the world has seemed to me more urgent than ever before. I have other sheep that are not of this fold (John 10:16). His outstretched Arms show us that He died for all, for *all*. No one is denied His love and forgiveness. My earthly day is drawing to a close. But Christ lives and the Church continues on her way. Oh the souls, the souls of men. May they be one! May they be one!

Chapter 8

THE JOY OF THE LORD

IN A GROUP DISCUSSION not long ago, a man asserted that he and his wife had committed their lives to Christ, as had one of their grown daughters.

"However, my other daughter," he said, "who is married and lives far from home, is not the least interested in God or anything pertaining to Him."

When I asked if he knew why this was so, he replied, "Because she and her husband love fun and gaiety. They are afraid if they become real Christians it will mean the end of the way of life they so enjoy."

What a tragic mistake it is to think that to follow Jesus, to commit one's life to Him, means the end of all fun and enjoyment. The life of the spirit is the most exciting life on earth; one never knows what is around the corner in the way of revelation. The individual who is open to God is continually being astonished at the marvelous things He has in store for each one of us, and at the thrilling and wonderful way in which He works out His plan in our lives. To attempt to walk in the spirit is not only exciting, but fun and sheer joy, as an increasing number of young people are discovering.

One of the most gratifying things to me in leading the ongoing ministry of healing at Calvary Episcopal Church has been the opportunity to watch people grow, not only in holiness, but in pure, unadulterated joy.

As we bid each other goodnight at the end of the service, each face is aglow as he or she tells me of blessings received; invariably there are a number who report healings that have occurred. The atmosphere is pervaded with thanksgiving and joy, for all there have asked in His name; they have received; and as He promised, their joy is full (John 16:24). The congregation is loath to leave the church, and as the people stand around in groups speaking together of the wonder of the living Christ, their happiness overflows.

This is not to say that the healing ministry has a monopoly on committed, joy-filled Christians; yet with few exceptions, those who believe in the healing Christ are uniquely and joyously dedicated. They have seen demonstrated the stupendous truth that the kingdom is not a matter of talk but of power (I Cor. 4:20 N.E.B.), and they know beyond the shadow of a doubt that Christ is a tremendous power within them (II Cor. 13:3 Phillips).

A young woman who lives in a midtown apartment house and comes regularly to the Calvary services told me of an episode that gladdened my heart. She said that when she had returned home from a healing service the preceding week, one of her neighbors happened to be sitting in the lobby as she walked in. The neighbor looked at her and remarked, "You must have been to a great party tonight, you look so happy. Where was it, anyway?"

When the reply young woman answered, "I was at the healing service at Calvary," her neighbor was astounded. To see someone come home from a church service radiant and bursting with joy seemed completely incredible.

Yet this is the way it *should* be. A long face and mournful demeanor is a travesty of Christianity. A doleful attitude has nothing whatsoever to do with reverence: It is a hangover from Puritanism, which has no rightful place, nor ever had, in the Christian faith. If our sins continue to crucify Christ, so must the dour, joyless Christian break the heart of God.

There was nothing "wrong" with that young woman who loved gaiety and parties. So, apparently did Jesus, as we remember Him at the wedding feast at Cana (John 2:1–10). Not only do we assume that He had a good time, but He wanted the guests to enjoy themselves also. When the wine ran out, He turned the water into wine, and the festivities continued unabated.

Saint Paul encourages us to enjoy all things. As he says, they have been given us by God, "Who giveth us richly all things to enjoy" (I Tim. 6:17). How sad it is that so many Christians seem to find so little to enjoy in God's good gifts. God calls us to be holy, yes; but holiness and joy should be synonymous for the Christian. Too often they are not, which is why a young woman who came to me for counseling rebelled when I suggested she attend healing services.

"I don't want to," she said. "Why should I go to a place filled with forbidding, 'holy' people, all miserable, sick and unhappy. I'm depressed enough myself," she continued, "without being subjected to *that* atmosphere."

I finally prevailed upon her at least to try a healing service. She quickly discovered how wrong she had been, and now she never misses a service. She found not "forbidding, 'holy'" people, but the joy of the Lord. She now lives in this joy and abundantly manifests it to others.

A number of people fly in from various states to attend the Calvary services, and without exception they have all expressed the very same thought in differing words: "I have never felt such joy and love as at this service. It is an experience I shall never forget." They have experienced the meaning of the fellowship of the people of God.

Christian joy goes far beyond pleasure, gaiety, and happiness, although it may well include all three; and it is not marked by a saccharine sweetness and a false and forced cheeriness. Many of us would agree with the British writer and theologian Charles Williams when he says, "There is an offensive cheerfulness encouraged by some Christians which is very trying to any person of moderate sensibility." [1]

True joy is one side of the Christian coin; on the other is suffering. Unless we share in the common suffering of the world which is also the suffering of our Lord, we cannot enter into His joy. The early Christians went to their deaths singing joyous hymns of praise. As it was their joy in the face of persecution and martydom which resulted in the conversion of many pagans two thousand years ago, so it is this same joy that effects conversion today. The unbeliever observes the committed Christian and says, "I want what he has," and "what he has," of course, is the Lord Jesus Christ.

"Rejoice in the Lord always, and again I say rejoice," Paul enjoins us (Phil. 4:4). These are words of healing, for in the joy of the Lord does indeed lie our strength (Neh. 8:10). It is this joy that undergirds all true worship, that leads us into heartfelt thanksgiving and ceaseless praise, that underlies our intercessions (for part of our joy is our knowledge that God hears and answers prayer). It underlies even our penitence, for there is inestimable joy in our certitude that He never fails to forgive.

"For the kingdom of God is not meat and drink; but righteousness, and peace, and joy in the Holy Ghost" (Rom. 14:17).

These three—righteousness (or at least our striving toward it), peace, and joy—are inseparable and indivisible, for peace without joy degenerates into mere passivity, and righteousness without joy becomes prideful arrogance.

"Except a man be born again, he cannot see the king-

[1] Charles Williams, *He Came Down from Heaven* (London: Faber and Faber, 1950), p. 96.

dom of God" (John 3:3), and the fullness of His joy can be found only within the kingdom—that kingdom which is at once within us and yet to come (Luke 17:21).

"How can a man be born again?" asked Nicodemus (John 3:4). We ask the same question today, and the answer is the same as that given two thousand years ago: "Except a man be born of water and of the Spirit," Jesus says, "he cannot enter into the kingdom of God" (John 3:5).

Here our Lord enunciates the formula of Christian baptism as He proclaims the necessity of a spiritual regeneration "of water and of the Spirit." In His reply to Nicodemus He seems to make it clear that such baptism is necessary for salvation. Thus the majority of churches teach that in the sacrament of baptism we *are* born again, cleansed of sin, spiritually regenerated by the action of the Holy Spirit, and made members of the Body of Christ.

None of the sacraments, including baptism, is magic. If, as is the custom in many of the established churches, we are baptized as infants and live our entire adult lives apart from God and in sin, the fact that we were baptized will not save us, nor will the fact that as baptized Christians we may give lukewarm assent to whatever portions of the gospel we choose to believe, live by the Golden Rule and attend church every Sunday. It is necessary, as our Lord made clear, that we be *consciously* aware that we have been born again, or more accurately, born from above of God.

What then is this rebirth experience? What actually happens, and how does it affect us?

For the purpose of simplification, rebirth can be equated with conversion. The two are not precisely the same, because the word "conversion" as we use it generally applies to someone who has never known Christ, while the new-birth experience applies most often to those who have known and believed in Him, but less

than completely. Nonetheless, conversion and rebirth
have much in common. When the experience of rebirth
occurs suddenly and dramatically there is an unforget-
table moment of glorious truth, occasioned by the strong
action of the Holy Spirit, when one accepts *entirely*—
not just with his mind, but with his heart and spirit and
his whole being—the stupendous fact that Jesus is indeed
his personal Saviour and Redeemer. It is in this moment
that the individual recognizes the extent of his sins, experiences the miracle of God's absolving grace, and
commits his life utterly and without reservation to his
Lord. The grace of the Holy Spirit, Whom you received
in baptism, is conveyed now in a new and fuller way.
You are enabled to claim, appropriate, exercise, and prepare to develop your relationship with God already established in baptism. If the new life in Christ is to be
lived, there must be a "new" creature to live it, and we
cannot become "new creatures" on our own; we must be
reborn by the power of the Spirit. This is the sort of rebirth Jesus was talking about to Nicodemus.

When this new birth takes place, the born-again Christian knows experientially the reality of God and of His
love, and the redemptive grace of Christ. He has appro-
priated the gift of the Holy Spirit promised by Saint Peter
(Acts 2:38, 39) and received in baptism. This experiential knowledge of your spirit given by the Spirit may
come in a variety of ways. Don't expect everyone's experience to be exactly like yours.

Very frequently there will be an exquisitely precise
moment of truth. If this happens to you, it will be an
experience without parallel in your life. It is in that moment that you will know not only with your mind but
with your heart the complete holiness of God: His love
for *you*, personally, and the lengths to which He has gone
to prove His love by His Crucifixion. You will find yourself overwhelmed with your love for *Him* and with sorrow for your sins. Your heart will cry, "Lord, forgive, I am

not worthy. Take me, all that I am, my life in its entirety, and use it as You will, for Your glory." You will simultaneously experience the greatest joy you have ever known. You will rise from your knees a new creature in Christ (II Cor. 5:17).

"Except a man be born again, he cannot see the kingdom of God." You have now been reborn, and you have glimpsed the kingdom. Your rebirth has happened within you, but it will be vividly apparent to all who know you.

Although the new-birth experience often occurs suddenly and dramatically, there are many for whom it is a gradual and scarcely perceptible awakening. These individuals cannot pinpoint in time the moment when they became aware of the reality of Jesus Christ and embraced not only His teachings but Himself. So far as they can remember, these persons have always known and accepted with joy their relationship with God. In other words, their baptism, at whatever age it occurred, "took."

It cannot be overemphasized that the born-again experience need not necessarily involve an instantaneous emotional reaction. I remember well a young woman who publicly committed her life to Christ at a Faith at Work religious conference. She came to me afterward, almost in tears, because she had not "felt" anything; she had heard no angels sing and no bells ring as she committed her life.

I saw this young woman over a year later. Just a few weeks before, she had experienced the sorrow for sin, the peace and indescribable joy, the experiential knowledge of Christ as her Saviour, which are characteristic of the born-again Christian. She was aglow with His radiance, and she said, "You know, my life is entirely different now."

Of course it was; old things had passed away, and all things had become new (II Cor. 5:17). She had been reborn into the joy of the Lord.

Each one of us experiences and is given to appropriate

in a different way that new life in Christ which became ours at baptism. The important thing to realize is this: Even if our born-again experience comes to us as a great flash of lightning, even if we know the precise instant when we were made new in Him, this experience is never a static thing. No Christian ever "has it made," for our "Yes" to Christ is a continuous and ongoing process that will never cease as long as we live.

"If thou shalt confess with thy mouth the Lord Jesus, and shalt believe in thine heart that God hath raised him from the dead, thou shalt be saved" (Rom. 10:9). This means far more than an exciting subjective religious experience, and it means far more than an intellectual assent to the fact that Christ was born, lived, was crucified, and rose again. It is only when the *heart* believes, and the *spirit* responds and *continues* to respond, that one is born from above.

It is worth noting that one of the outstanding characteristics of the healing ministry which is in no small part responsible for the power released and the joy experienced during healing services is the predominantly large number of reborn Christians associated with this ministry. The reason for this is not difficult to determine: Christ is within us (immanent) and at the same time outside us (transcendent). In a special way and with unique vividness, we confront the living God at the altars of His healing church. One cannot experience such a confrontation without being born anew in Him; and one cannot emerge from such a confrontation without becoming, in some way, a new creature.

It is through the new birth experience, wherever, whenever, and however it may come about, that we enter into the joy of the Lord. Believing now in a new way with a new fervency, we "rejoice with joy unspeakable" (I Pet. 1:8). With the Psalmist we say, and mean it with all our being, "In thy presence is fulness of joy; at thy right hand there are pleasures for evermore" (Ps. 16:11).

Chapter 9

"WILT THOU BE MADE WHOLE?"

AMONG THE FACTORS that inhibit God's healing power is one so prevalent, so important, and withal so insidious, that it deserves a chapter to itself. I refer to the lack of desire to be healed. To fail to *want* to be well is in itself a sickness, which has its scriptural counterpart in the gospel account of the healing of the man at Bethesda (John 5:2–17).

Here we see an ill person who gives Jesus one flimsy excuse after another as to why he has not been healed. Our Lord immediately understands the true situation and asks of the sick man, "Wilt thou be made whole?" (John 5:6)—in other words, "Do you *want* to be well again?"

This is a question I believe many ailing people must ask themselves today and search their hearts for an honest answer. "But," you may be thinking, "surely no one can *want* to be sick, or hold resentments, or suffer from poor relationships either at home or in business."

Unfortunately, as I have learned over the years, a great many people who ostensibly seek healing for whatever brokenness may exist in their lives *do* want things to re-

main precisely as they are. They do *not* honestly want
themselves or the situation healed. This lack of real desire to have their lives made whole is usually unconscious, and therefore such individuals frequently need
outside help to bring it to their conscious awareness.

But bringing it to their conscious mind is only the
first step. From there on the major and most important
portion of their healing consists in changing their frame
of mind so that they truly desire health and wholeness.
This is the most difficult part of the healing, but by
God's grace it can be achieved. Once a person sincerely
wants to be made whole in Christ's name and for His
sake, the healing is virtually accomplished. The ailment to which he has clung, perhaps for years, whether it
be physical, mental, or emotional, is very apt to quickly
disappear.

A typical example concerns a woman who, when she
was widowed, went to live with her daughter and son-in-
law. They loved her deeply and genuinely wanted her
with them. They owned a large house where she could be
made comfortable and enjoy, both for their sakes and her
own, a modicum of privacy.

This woman was not elderly. She was in her middle
fifties, and her health had previously been excellent.
However, within a few weeks after moving into her
daughter's home, she began to ail. She became miserably
and genuinely ill, although her physician could find
nothing organically wrong with her. She finally came to
the point where she had to spend most of her time in bed.
She could eat virtually nothing without suffering acute
discomfort, became very weak, and suffered from almost
total insomnia. (Let me remark here that whether an illness is psychosomatic or organic makes no difference so
far as suffering is concerned. Psychosomatic illness is just
as real, just as painful, just as incapacitating, as organic
sickness.)

It was this woman's daughter and son-in-law who, greatly concerned, asked me to see her. By the end of our first session, I felt I had put my finger on the problem. Like any widow under similar circumstances, she had formerly run her own home, in her case for more than thirty years. The adjustment to living in someone else's house was a difficult one: perhaps more difficult for her because she was extremely determined that she not be accused of "interfering." She was therefore under constant tension, fearful of expressing any contrary opinion. It was an unnatural and inhibited way of life, which no one could live indefinitely without detriment.

Now these things were contributing factors to her condition, but they were not the real reason for her sickness. The real reason was this: The most difficult adjustment a widow or a widower has to make is to the fact that no matter how devoted the children or grandchildren, no matter how loving other relatives and friends, a bereaved spouse is no longer first in anyone's life. The woman I speak of simply had not been able to make this most difficult emotional adjustment.

In talking with me she was embarrassed and apologetic; she blamed no one but herself. With her rational mind she would have had it no other way, but emotionally she had been unable to accept the fact that, as much as her daughter loved her, the daughter's husband had to come first in her life.

This woman had not been an overly possessive or demanding mother, but now, in an unconscious effort to come first in someone's life, she had become ill in order to focus attention on herself. She did not *want* to be well, for if she were, she felt she would be of less concern to her children.

This was clear to me from the beginning, but not to her, and had I pointed it out on that first visit she would have vehemently denied it. She might well have become angry and hostile toward me, most likely refusing to see me again, and thus I would have been powerless to help her. I prayed with her that first afternoon without laying on hands, asking the guidance of the Holy Spirit for both of us.

During the next few weeks the burden of my prayer at home for her was not for her physical cure, but that her neurosis might be healed by the love of God so that she would truly *want* to be well.

I saw her over a period of some six weeks, and toward the end of our last conference, she broke down and cried, she *herself* admitted what I had felt to be the trouble the first time I saw her.

During that final session together we prayed, this time with the laying on of hands, asking God to heal the brokenness of her spirit, praying that God's love would be so real to her that she would no longer need to feel "first" among those on earth. Our prayer was answered with a great affirmation of a Christian truth: that although God has so many millions of children, each one of us is to Him as special as though he were His only child —and, as such, all-important in His sight.

Within days this woman was amazingly better. Within two weeks, although formerly an irregular churchgoer, she began to attend church each Sunday and a healing service once a week. She is well now, but continues (as she should) to attend weekly healing services. She does this for several reasons, among them because, as she puts it, "When I receive the laying on of hands, it is as though our Lord Himself is touching me. I know the reality of His presence and His love at healing services as at no other time. I know there that I am His."

There are many like this woman who subconsciously do not want to be healed; but there are also some who, not understanding the healing ministry, *dare* not seek the healing power of God. There are those who suffer

from a medically incurable disease, and with enormous
spiritual effort have made peace with their situation. They
are afraid to seek Christ's healing touch lest they not be
physically cured. They cannot face the prospect of fighting all over again the battle of acceptance they have
already won. In cases like this, I suggest that, except for
private prayer, well-meaning enthusiasts of the healing
ministry do not interfere.

To the question "Wilt thou be made whole?", which I
seldom ask directly, I often add *very* directly, "Why do
you want to be healed? What will you do with your life
if you *are* healed?"

Not long ago I asked this of a woman whose arm,
broken ten weeks before, was not healing. Her answer
came swiftly, and, I thought, a little too glibly. "I'll
devote the rest of my life to the glory of God," she said.

Week after week she came to the Calvary healing services, and I could see no evidence of either physical or
spiritual healing taking place.

The last time she counseled with me she spoke continually of a trip to Europe she had long planned and
now would have to cancel. Suddenly I found myself
saying, "Look, let's examine your motives. Do you really
want to be healed so that God will be glorified, or so that
you can go to Europe?"

She looked nonplused for a moment, then burst out: "I
want that trip to Europe more than anything else in the
world. I couldn't care less about the glory of God!"

Here then was the trouble spot. It was not so much that
her motives were wrong as that she had been dishonest
with God—for it is honesty that He honors, not a false
piety. That day she prayed with me, telling God how she
really felt. Obviously, *He* did not need this information,
but *she* needed to give it. The result? Her arm healed
within ten days, and she went to Europe as planned,
overwhelmed with gratitude to God. I heard from others

that throughout the trip she made a moving and powerful witness to her Lord.

"Wilt thou be made whole?" Surely implicit in our Lord's question to the man at Bethesda was "How *much* do you want to be well?"

This is the question I am still asking a businessman who claims he wants to be healed, but apparently not sufficiently to remove the barriers which are impeding the inflow of God's healing grace.

This man, in his forties, has worked for the same firm for many years. Two years ago he was passed over for a promotion which he believed he merited. He is particularly bitter because the man who is now his superior had a drinking problem. Had it not been for the man I am counseling, who covered for his boss again and again, the man would have lost his job instead of being promoted. This is an understandable reason for resentment on the part of the subordinate, but he makes no effort to release it; rather, he appears to embrace it. The resentment has, in a sense, become a reason for his being. When I have tried to point out how he is harming himself, his reply is "Yes—but it is only human to resent this injustice."

Exactly so, which is why we must continually strive to be rid of such human sins of the spirit, and this can only be done by opening our hearts to the supranatural love and grace of God. This man initially came to me seeking healing for a physical ailment, but thus far I have been unable to help him, for he has shut himself off from God's healing power. God coerces no one, and this man, for the time being, has freely chosen to take no corrective measures, but instead to make his resentment a way of life. I am still working with him, confident that in the end the healing Christ will triumph, that in due time his spiritual ears will be unstopped and his spiritual eyes opened, that he may hear and see the truth.

Not long ago, he said with a grin, "You never give up, do you?" No, I don't, for at long last I have learned patience—an attribute which as Christians we should all try to cultivate, for we are dealing not only with the now but with all eternity. Great patience is particularly necessary for people who reject their healings, for whatever reason: Patience will allow them time for self-examination, and if required, extensive counseling, so that they may learn to live in a climate conducive to healing.

Once we have learned this, we all may be assured that we are growing, however slowly, in grace and holiness. We all can be certain that we shall be healed spiritually, so that we may truly want to be well. When that time comes, the chances are excellent that we shall receive the healing of which we are in need, whether it be physical, mental, or emotional.

Many of us would agree with Saint Teresa that patience is near the top of the list of Christian virtues, and that the painfulness of its acquisition is one of mankind's greatest crosses. Particularly is this true of us who live in this day and age, for we are members of what is probably the most impatient era in history. We are a generation of "instant" everything, from instant coffee to instant religious experience. However, there is no short cut to the fulfillment of the kingdom of God. The road to holiness is a long one, and we do not stop traveling when we are healed. We continue along it for the rest of our lives, blessed every step of the way by the Light of the world, by whom the path is lit.

It is true of all of us, and particularly of those who at one time may have rejected His healing grace, that once having tasted God, we are impatient and eager for more; there is born in us that holy desire which comes from God. But we cannot receive all of Him all at once, or indeed all of Him ever on this earth. He in His wisdom gives us what we can handle at a given time. Too much too soon can dangerously unbalance us emotionally.

Therefore, cultivate assiduously that fruit of the spirit called patience (Gal. 5:22 Jer.). When you seek healing, make sure you really want to be healed. If you even faintly suspect that in your heart you are enjoying your illness, or if you know that you are clinging to a sin of the spirit, ask God to release you from it. Pray that He will heal your spirit, and instill in you a genuine desire to be whole. He will answer your prayer, and the chances are good that your physical healing will follow.

Finally, be honest with God concerning your motive for healing. Don't pray piously, in a bargaining spirit: "Please, God, heal me, and I'll give you my life," when what you really mean is, "Heal me, God, so that I can go to that party two weeks from Saturday."

When you are unsure of your motives, one of the most effective prayers for healing I know, taken from the Book of Common Prayer, is, "Almighty God, unto whom all hearts are open, all desires known, and from whom no secrets are hid; Cleanse the thoughts of our hearts by the inspiration of thy Holy Spirit, that we may perfectly love thee, and worthily magnify thy Holy Name, through Christ our Lord." If we pray this prayer frequently and sincerely, we are likely to hear in our hearts the words of Jesus that were spoken to the sick man at Bethesda: "Rise, take up thy bed, and walk" (John 5:8).

And very likely it shall be with us, as it was with him: "And immediately the man was made whole, and took up his bed, and walked" (John 5:9).

Chapter 10

FAITH AND
THE KINGDOM

"HOW CAN I ACQUIRE the faith necessary for healing?" is a perpetual question and at times one of obsessive concern to those to whom the healing ministry is new (or not so new, for that matter).

A simplistic answer is "You can't acquire faith; it is a gift of God. Your task is merely to appropriate that already-given gift."

But how do you do this? The first step is to realize the nature of faith, for the word "faith" is bandied about by all and sundry as though it were some sort of magic formula that of itself can heal. The fact is that faith of itself never healed anyone. It is God who heals, and faith that releases His power in our lives.

"What must I do to be saved?" asked the jail keeper of Paul and Silas (Acts 16:30). The reply came swiftly: "Believe on the Lord Jesus Christ." Substitute the word *healed* for *saved* in the question, and the answer is the same: Believe on the Lord Jesus Christ.

His miracles, accomplished by the power of the Holy

Spirit both when He walked the earth and today, are acts of mercy and evidence of His compassion. They are also signs witnessing to the kingdom He came to bring in. This is why He cannot work miracles unless He finds that quality of faith without which the signs and wonders, both two thousand years ago and now, lose their significance.

The possession of miracle-working faith demands in so far as is humanly possible the yielding of the whole person to God. This in turn requires an act of humility very difficult to perform, especially among us "do-it-yourself" Americans. Many people decline to make this act; more attempt it in half-hearted fashion, wanting the crown of healing without the cross of self-surrender. And total surrender to almighty God is a cross on which we must continually crucify ourselves if we are to be able to say with Saint Paul: "Not I, but Christ, liveth in me" (Gal. 2:20).

Some months ago a man came to me who had staggering problems, emotional, physical, and spiritual. At the same time, his marriage was on the rocks. He went to church regularly, knew his Scripture with his mind but not with his heart, and he was quick to admit that he was only a lip-service Christian. But he had a truly sincere desire to know his Lord.

"I *want* to believe with my heart that Jesus is my Lord and Saviour," he said, "but I just can't. My mind gets in the way no matter how hard I try."

This man actually spoke for many, and I tried to explain as I have so often before that in the area of faith, as in all other areas of our spiritual lives, it is our *wills* that God wants first. If we *will* to believe in our Lord with all our hearts, and if our overriding desire is for more of God, He will honor our will and desire for total commitment to Him.

To this man I submitted a plan for his consideration

that has proved extremely effective for countless individuals. I submit it here for you, for whether your faith is strong or weak, this is an exercise which I believe all of us could undertake with benefit once or twice a year.

Surround yourself as much as possible with believers; try to affiliate yourself with a prayer group; and attend healing services regularly, for here you will find yourself in an atmosphere of almost palpable faith. Then undertake what I call the thirty-day experiment of faith. For a period of one month act and live the promises of Jesus as if you believed with the unqualified fervency of the early Christians.

For thirty days, awaken each morning with His name on your lips. Before getting out of bed, offer Him praise and thanksgiving for another day, and offer Him your life for that day, praying that the Holy Spirit will guide you in all you do and say.

For thirty days, pray regularly, if only for a few minutes, morning, noon, and night, and throughout the day observe the presence of God by frequently offering brief sentence-prayers of praise.

For thirty days, read fifteen minutes a day of the New Testament, always asking first the guidance of the Holy Spirit. Read with special care of our Lord's healing miracles, as if you really *believed* that He is the same yesterday, today, and forever (He. 13:8). Read all of the First Epistle of Saint John each week. This is a short epistle, and so filled with the love of God that no one who reads it under the guidance of the Spirit can fail to respond.

Before going to sleep at night, ask the forgiveness of God for any sin you may have committed, and *believe* that you are forgiven. Finally, ask yourself whether you have done one thing that day because *He* said to do it, or whether that day you have abstained from one thing because He said *not* to do it. I suggest this final exercise for an important reason: It is a curious thing that while true faith leads to obedience, the converse is likewise true —obedience leads to a viable faith.

Live by the tiny light you have, which may be only your *desire* for faith in the Lord Jesus, and you will receive increasingly more. Cardinal Newman once said, "To all who wish for light, but cannot find it, one precept must be given: OBEY." I have seen the validity of these words confirmed again and again.

During this period of thirty days, you will probably be assaulted by such thoughts as, "This is silly. I don't need this; my faith is strong enough." Or, "This is ridiculous. I don't believe any of it." Whatever form these assaults take, praise God for them, for the closer you come to Him, the more violently Satan will assail you with such thoughts. Be firm with your "Get thee behind me, Satan," and continue on your way, unafraid to pray, "Lord, I believe; help thou mine unbelief." No matter how strong our faith, there are few of us who do not occasionally cry out to God with this prayer. God will honor it, as He did when the father of a sick boy spoke it nearly two thousand years ago (Mark 9:24). But, now as then, He still wants to hear those first words: "Lord, I believe."

At the end of the month, if your desire to believe wholly in Christ has been strong and sincere, you are virtually assured of finding yourself with an undaunted faith and the courage to claim His promises in your own life. He will honor your faith, and your life will be transfigured.

So it was with the man I mentioned earlier. At the end of the allotted thirty days, he found (somewhat to his own surprise) that he actually *did* believe with his heart those things that before he had said only with his lips. He still had his anxieties and apprehensions, but they had lessened and now he could cope with them. Today he is a truly committed Christian. His spiritual life is strong; his marriage has been restored by the love of Christ he now manifests; and his deep-seated emotional difficulties are a thing of the past. He has learned the verity of the words "This is the victory which overcometh the world, even our faith" (I John 5:4).

He is still not completely healed physically, although he is much improved. As he awaits the complete healing of his body, he says, "It no longer seems to really matter to me whether I am physically healed or not. What *does* matter are the things I now know: that Jesus is *my* Saviour; the reality of His love, and the fact that He is always with me." Such an attitude is always cause for rejoicing, for it indicates true wholeness—the kind that matters most—and it also goes a long way toward assuring physical healing.

This man continues to attend healing services, after asking so common a question that it is worth mentioning here.

"Isn't it a lack of faith," he wondered, "to continue to pray for healing after praying once and then committing oneself to God?"

The answer to this question is an emphatic "No." Our Lord's admonition is to pray persistently—and to faint not (Luke 18:1). Again and again He gives us parables to illustrate how God honors persevering prayer, such as the stories of the friend at midnight (Luke 11:5-8) and the importunate widow (Luke 18:1-8).

Persevering prayer, far from denoting lack of faith, is an act of obedience to our Lord. Coming to Him again and again in expectancy demonstrates not faltering, but rather an unshakable and unswerving faith in the goodness and mercy of God, who has assured us that "him that cometh to me I will in no wise cast out" (John 6:37).

This coming to God is repeatedly emphasized throughout the New Testament, and especially in the Lord's Prayer. Here we ask, "Give us this day our daily bread"; we don't pray once a year for a twelve months' supply. We cannot store up God's grace. He wants us to come to Him continually. We don't, for example, receive holy communion once in a lifetime, for we cannot bank the grace received. We partake of His Body and Blood again and again.

In the healing ministry we respond to His call, "Come unto Me," on a continuous and continuing basis. At first we may go a little hesitantly, not quite sure what is involved. Our courage increases, and each time, by the leading of the Spirit, we come a little closer to Him, until at last we come boldly unto the throne of grace (Heb. 4:16). Standing now on holy ground, we begin to understand the meaning of it all. To Him who has known us before the foundation of the world (Eph. 1:4, 5), we offer our entire beings, having recognized Him at long last. As we now call Him by name and prostrate ourselves in adoration at His feet, He extends His hand and blesses us, and we are made whole.

I believe it behooves us all to examine the true nature of faith. You have not real faith until you can say and mean it, "Though he slay me, yet will I put my trust in him" (Job 13:15). You have not real faith if you say, as I heard a minister say of a woman dying of cancer, "If she recovers, I'll believe in the power of God to heal." Faith is not dependent upon signs. You have not a real understanding of faith if, your own body touched by the healing Christ, you look at another who is not physically perfect and say, "If he had *my* faith, he would be healed." For as many unbelievers are healed (through the faith of others), so are many of the faithful physically unhealed, though never left untouched by His healing hand.

I think often of a religious conference I happened

to attend. At the conference was a little woman, crippled from birth, who had long ago committed her life to Christ. She attends healing services regularly, praying always for others, and that God will use her life for His glory.

I was greatly disturbed when at the conference I happened to overhear someone say to her, in a tone both condescending and arrogant, "If you really believed in God, you'd be healed. Look at *me*. I was healed because I had faith."

Later that night, the devout and holy little woman came to me in tears. "But I *do* believe in God," she said, "and I know He can heal. Does the fact that I limp mean there's something wrong with my faith?"

After talking with her for a while, we prayed together, and she left reassured. And that night I prayed fervently for the person who had made that remark. So much harm, so much unnecessary suffering, is caused by the ignorance and insensitivity of those who profess to be working in the name of Christ and witnessing for His sake.

Everyone who believes in the Lord Jesus is saved, but he is not always physically healed. We do not know why, but we are sure that the failure is not necessarily due to a personal lack of deep faith. We base our certainty not only on the teaching of the ancient church—which placed the responsibility for failure to heal on herself, as the Body—but also on the Scripture from which this teaching was derived. For although our Lord frequently said to the one healed, "Thy faith hath made thee whole," He also healed the multitudes, many of whom, it is safe to assume, did not hold an intense personal faith. To be sure, He made clear that faith *somewhere* is necessary, whether it be the faith of friends, of the group as a whole, or of the one who ministers. While we cannot ever underestimate the value of the faith of one who seeks healing, we must also note that Jesus did not always demand personal faith. He did not, for example, demand faith of Malchus, when He healed the ear of the servant of the high priest (Luke 22:50, 51), and it is highly unlikely that this man believed he would be healed.

Nor did Jesus mention the faith of the man with palsy brought to the Great Physician by his friends (Mark 2:3–5). So crowded was the house where Jesus was that the sick man's friends could not get him near our Lord, so they let down the bed of the invalid through the roof. We are told that when Jesus saw the faith of the sick man's *friends*, He said, "Son, thy sins are forgiven thee," and the man with palsy was healed. Jesus did not mention *his* faith (or lack of it), only the faith of his friends.

When persons come to me, as did a woman not long ago, saying, "Please help me achieve faith so I can be healed," I am given pause to think. In our too-often harassed and frenetic efforts to "achieve" faith, we are putting the cart before the horse. In a very real sense, it is Christ and not faith we should be seeking.

"I live now not with my own life but with the life of Christ who lives in me," says Saint Paul. Therefore it follows, as the apostle says, that "the life I now live in this body, I live in faith" (Gal. 2:20 Jer.). This means simply that if you are aware that Christ lives in you, you have all the faith you can possibly need, for Christ *is* your faith.

The ancient church sought Christ and Christ alone, and as a result great miracles followed. And so it is today: Miracles occur in direct proportion to the fervency with which we seek our Lord. *Your* miracle of healing will occur in one form or another if your quest is Christ for His sake, and not faith for faith's sake.

Chapter 11

PREPARING THE CLIMATE FOR HEALING

As WE ARE NEVER out of God's love, so are we never beyond the reach of His healing hand. He longs to restore us to wholeness; to heal our ailing bodies, our tormented minds, our alienated spirits, our broken relationships. In short, He yearns to heal us even more than we long to be healed.

Although we may not know why everyone is not healed, we do know something of the conditions which, generally speaking, must be met if we are to be made whole. We know the necessity of establishing and living in a spiritual climate which will best enable us to receive His healing power, and above all Himself.

It is perfectly true that during our Lord's earthly ministry He healed all who came to Him: "And great multitudes followed Him and He healed them all" (Matt. 12:15). It seems obvious that Jesus did not tell the people who followed Him that they had to establish a particular "climate" for healing. He simply saw their need, and He met it.

Why, then, you may wonder, do we emphasize the

necessity of such a climate today? Simply because we are living in an era of unparalleled unbelief that extends even into the church. We are assailed on all sides by the knowledge of men, which seeks to obscure the wisdom of God. We need a climate for healing not for God's sake, that He may then consent to make us whole, but for *our* sakes, that we may more readily receive that which He stands so ready to give.

To prepare such a climate we must first rid ourselves, with God's help, of those factors within ourselves which lock our hearts against Him. Asking the guidance of the Holy Spirit, we examine ourselves, seeking to find, to recognize, and to call by name, those sins that separate us from Him. We may well not be guilty of any overt sins, but we may find ourselves surprised at the resentments, jealousies, envy, feelings of hostility, and similar sins of the spirit that we are harboring—all of which set up a barrier to the inflow of Christ's life in our lives.

After a general preliminary examination of ourselves, which is the first step toward establishing the climate for healing, and after a brief daily self-examination (which should be limited to three or four minutes to avoid morbid introspection), it is enough to pray, "Search me, O God, and know my heart: try me and know my thoughts: and see if there be any wicked way in me" (Ps. 139:3, 4); "Wash me thoroughly from mine iniquity, and cleanse me from my sin" (Ps. 51:2).

Little by little those spiritual sins that may be separating us from God and hindering His healing power will be unearthed. The next step is to get rid of them, which is often far from easy.

In another book I have submitted some concrete suggestions in the form of certain symbolic acts accompanied by prayer, which have proved helpful to many.[1]

[1] Emily Gardiner Neal, *Where There's Smoke* (New York: Morehouse-Barlow, 1967), p. 151.

As one more example of such an act, I cite the recent experience of a young clergyman who wrote me in real distress, saying that for the first time in his life he felt not only resentment but actual hatred against a certain individual. He had prayed hard and long but apparently to no avail, and finally in desperation he had written to me for help. Before I had time to answer this letter, I received another, this time an exuberant one, telling me that he was now completely liberated from his destructive emotion.

He had devised his own "act." He had written a letter expressing all that he felt: the hostility, the hate, the anger. He had sealed the letter with Scotch tape and put it in the back of an unused drawer; he locked the drawer and then threw away the key. This was a symbolic gesture of "putting away" his hate. It was a sacramental act, an outward and visible sign of an inward and spiritual intention that the love of God fill him once again. It worked. The hate was gone, locked out of his life; the entire situation was overtaken by God's love.

No two people are alike, and no one method is helpful to all individuals. I remember well the woman who came to me announcing that she was going to leave her husband. She was filled with bitterness against the man to whom she had been married for twenty-five years. Their life together was filled with bickering, hostility, and general incompatibility. I talked with her many times and from the human point of view, the situation appeared hopeless. After praying each time we were together that Christ's love might overshadow this marriage and restore all brokenness, I told her that I would not see her again until she agreed to hold up her husband each day in the love of Christ, asking God to bless him, asking forgiveness for her inability to love (however justified this inability might seem), and praying that God would enable her to love as He did.

One day, about three months later, she came to me and with wonderment in her voice said, "You know, I prayed as you told me for a long time. Then suddenly one day I realized I hadn't prayed that way for weeks. I realized that it wasn't because I had *forgotten*, but that it was no longer necessary. God had answered me, and I had come at last to really love my husband."

The next week she attended a healing service to offer thanksgiving for her happy marriage.

One of the vital conditions for healing in every area of our lives consists of forgiveness: the forgiveness of God toward us and our forgiveness toward those who have wronged us—or those whom we *think* have wronged us, which as far as we are concerned, amounts to the same thing. "Forgive us our trespasses as we forgive those who trespass against us." Unless we forgive others, God cannot forgive us, for unless we have first forgiven, we have within us a wall of bitterness and resentment that closes us off from God. If we are to receive Him and His healing grace, we must become open channels through which His power can flow—and lack of forgiveness on our parts clogs that channel with particles of resentment, or envy or hate or self-pity. These constitute the cholesterol of the soul. The dissolvent for this spiritual cholesterol is forgiveness.

"Forgive us our trespasses as we forgive those who trespass against us." These words tended to puzzle me years ago. They seemed to imply the attitude, "All right, Lord. See how magnanimous I am to forgive so-and-so. Therefore You must now forgive me."

One day I realized that the whole basis of forgiveness is love, and what this phrase from the Lord's Prayer really meant was: "We know Your forgiveness, Lord. Please help us to forgive like that."

As in our relationship with God *He* was the first to love—"We love God because He first loved us" (I John

4:19)—so likewise He was the first to forgive: He died on the cross for our sins. So although we must forgive others if God is to be able to forgive us, yet it is God who has performed the first and great act of forgiveness. It is through Him, and by His grace alone, that we are enabled to forgive.

The best way I know to help us forgive those who have trespassed against us is to think of what Christ has done for us. If we fail to accept in our hearts the fact that we are pardoned sinners, if we fail to live in the knowledge of God's merciful forgiveness, we ourselves cannot possibly forgive.

Once having learned to forgive, and by God's grace gotten rid of those factors that hinder His healing power in our lives, the soil for healing is prepared. But there are still conditions to be met before the climate is established.

There is, for example, that attitude of thanksgiving which is an essential element of the healing climate. It is easy enough to be thankful when all goes well, but perhaps we cannot know the full meaning of thanksgiving until things have gone badly. In my own experience it has been within the context of pain that I have learned best how to be truly thankful—and for such prosaic things as I had always before taken for granted.

For over two and a half years, for example, I was unable to sit upright with my legs outstretched. This meant that I could not take a hot bath, and anyone with a bad back knows the relief afforded by a tub of hot water. The first time I was able to lower myself into a bathtub still stands out in my memory as a momentous event, and I have never forgotten my inexpressible gratitude to God. Every single day since that memorable occasion, as I step into a hot bath I fervently thank God that I am able to do so. Such a small thing, but for me it was, and still is, a minor miracle!

No matter how bad things may be, we can always

find something to be thankful for. The continual offering of our thanksgiving for things great and small becomes habitual with practice. When it becomes habitual, we have established an attitude indispensable to healing, whether of mind, body, or spirit.

Then there is the matter of obedience, which, like love, is an indispensable element in the climate of healing. It is obedience that leads us to the kingdom, obedience that springs from love. It is out of love—the love we bear for Christ—that we are constrained to obey. "If a man love me, he will keep my words," our Lord says (John 14:23).

We obey His words not out of fear, not for any reward that we think may result, but purely and simply out of love. As Saint Peter says, we ought to obey God rather than man, and the Holy Ghost is given to them that obey Him (Acts 5:29, 32). As the Holy Spirit is God active in our lives, without Him we are utterly helpless, without strength or life.

Whether or not we *understand* why He commands us to do certain things matters not at all. What *does* matter is that we do what He tells us to do. "Whatsoever he saith unto you, do it," said the Virgin Mary (John 2: 5). She was a perfect example of human obedience, which it behooves us all to follow.

The task of any Christian is simply to obey the divine command. His comfort, His strength, His healing, are always there, but our reception of them is dependent upon His grace, which He liberally bestows upon His obedient servants. Obedience is the cost of receiving in our lives that gift without price—something of the power of the living God. It is the cost if we are to receive the greatest of all blessings, an experiential knowledge of the risen, healing Christ.

Finally, I would mention trust, which is the other side of the coin of faith, and an intrinsic part of a total faith.

For it is quite possible to have a dynamic faith in God and still lack that quiet trust in Him which is essential to the healing climate.

To the precise extent that we trust Him we are enabled to live in His peace, without fear for today or apprehension for the future. "Thou wilt keep him in perfect peace, whose mind is stayed on Thee; because he trusteth in Thee" (Isa. 26:3). Self-reliance is considered a highly commendable virtue in our culture, but unless we are willing to substitute God-dependence for self-reliance, we can never claim this promise, nor can we ever know the meaning of true security. Until we learn to put our complete trust in Him, we will never comprehend His words, "My own peace I give you, a peace the world cannot give" (John 14:27); and failing to understand, we will be unable to appropriate one of His greatest gifts.

Many inquire about the need and method of preparation before attending a specific healing service. In my experience, there is great need for spiritual preparation before the service as well as during the service itself, which by including prayers of praise, thanksgiving, confession, and Scripture reading is a corporate reaffirmation of that preparation which has gone before. Whether one is attending a healing mission or regular weekly healing services, the preparation is ideally the same.

First comes fasting, which I believe to be invaluable. To do without food quickens the spirit, making the individual more receptive to the power of God (or if he is attending a service as intercessor, a more open channel for His healing grace). When the disciples asked Jesus why they had been unable to cast out an evil spirit, He replied, "This kind can come forth by nothing, but by prayer and fasting" (Mark 9:29). And so it seems today with many illnesses.

Prepare yourself before the service by much prayer,

predominantly of praise and thanksgiving. Examine your conscience and ask forgiveness for anything amiss in your life. Read Scripture, especially the accounts of some of the healing miracles. If time allows, do some spiritual reading. Attempt, in so far as you are able, to live those hours before the healing service in the spirit, in an attitude of prayer and meditation.

As more supplicants have learned the value of this prior preparation, the healing power of God has been increasingly manifested; this in turn has increased the faith of the church.

Chapter 12

LIVING IN
THE CLIMATE

HAVING PREPARED THE CLIMATE FOR HEALING, the next step is learning to live in that climate. It is the same atmosphere, actually, in which all who call themselves Christians might well endeavor to live, for "were you not taught the truth as it is in Jesus? You must be made new in mind and spirit, and put on the new nature of God's creating, which shows itself in the just and devout life" (Eph. 4:20–24 N.E.B.).

This "just and devout life," which is the Christian way as well as the climate for healing, is characterized by love and joy and peace, by praise and thanksgiving. To live in this way is *being* a Christian, with His life in you. This means not merely trying to follow Christ, it means to belong to Him with your entire self, body, mind, and spirit. To be such a Christian (not solely to attempt to live as one) means complete joy, a joy that permeates to the innermost depths of our being.

To be a Christian does not mean that we shall never

know pain or trouble or sickness. It does mean that we need never suffer from complete despair. For we know it is as Saint Paul says: Nothing can ever separate us from the love of God, and in all things, tribulation and distress, persecution and peril, we are more than conquerors through Him that loves us (Rom. 8:35).

Are these just pious words? I used to think so, and I remember how irritably I had said before I became a Christian, "It's just plain stupid to expect anyone to be joyous or thankful if he is sick or in pain or bereaved."

I have thought of that remark many times over the past years, when events in my own life gave them the lie. I recently thought of it again when an old friend who is still an agnostic said to me, "Are you honestly happier now as a Christian?"

My reply was a spontaneous "Of course! I never knew before what real joy was."

That I could make such a response seems to me a miracle in itself; for even as I spoke, there flashed through my mind the things that have happened to me since I embraced the faith. I felt once again, as I feel it so often, that welling up of thanksgiving that when these things *had* happened, I had *been* a Christian—for without Christ I would have been destroyed.

The more of God we are able to receive, the greater our wholeness, for in Him we possess those elements that comprise the climate of healing: an ever-increasing love and joy; the growing desire to praise and worship; the greatful heart that in time habitually offers thanksgiving regardless of outward circumstances.

These factors are the involuntary result of the risen Christ in our lives; at the same time, they constitute the spiritual laws that most of us break again and again. With most of us it is as Saint Paul says: "For what I would, that do I not; but what I hate, that do I" (Rom. 7:15).

I recall all too vividly how one night at dinner my husband and I were discussing someone who had done a grave injustice to one of our children.

"I hate her so much I could kill her!" I burst out.

Later that night, when alone in the house, ironing, I seemed actually to hear the words, so strongly were they impressed upon my heart: "Whosoever looketh on a woman to lust after her hath committed adultery with her already in his heart" (Matt. 5:28).

I remembered then what I had said at the dinner table. Not only had I broken the law of love, but I had broken the sixth commandment, for I had committed murder in my heart. Not even stopping to set the iron upright, I dropped to my knees and offered Him my contrite spirit. I still remember, years later, the healing of God's absolving grace as it washed over me. And I still have the scorched pillow case I was ironing at the time, to serve as a reminder.

As Saint Paul says, we all sin and we all break at one time or another one or more of the spiritual laws of healing, thus polluting the climate in which we are trying to live. But God stands always ready in His never-failing mercy to forgive and restore us, so the atmosphere in which we strive to live is cleansed and purified once more.

The perfect climate of healing, which few of us can attain but which it is our holy obligation continually to attempt to create and then live in, requires the most difficult of all things for most of us: the death of self. This final act is one that our Lord demands of all who make an effort to follow Him.

"If any man will come after me," He says, "let him deny himself, and take up his cross and follow me" (Matt. 16:24).

Jesus did not mean by "denying" oneself to give up

some material pleasure one might desire; He meant that
we must renounce ourselves. This renunciation of self
is a continual struggle, but a joyful one, in which we
engage purely out of the love we bear for Him to Whom
we offer our lives; it is a battle whose victory lies in
unconditional surrender. It means the alignment of our
wills with His, so that there are not two wills—His and
ours—but one will: His.

It means a daily (perhaps hourly) "funeral" of self; but
it is a "white" funeral and therefore a gloriously triumphant one. We know that only when we are dead to
self can we be empty of self and thus be filled by God.

There are probably few of us who work publicly in the
healing ministry who have not been told from time to
time by people in the congregation that as we were
speaking, there was visible above our heads a nimbus, a
circle of radiant light. Some time ago a phenomenon
was reported to me that I treasure above all else that
has happened during a healing service, for from it I
learned so invaluable a lesson.

It was the final service of a very strenuous mission,
and by the time that last service came, I was exhausted
and my back so painful that I wondered how I could ever
get through it. Just before it was time to speak, I remember praying, "Lord, take from me all desire except that Thy
most holy will may be done this night. Empty me of
self, and fill me with Thyself. This time, Lord, please
speak not only *through* me but *for* me."

As I stepped into the pulpit, I was conscious of a
surge of supernatural strength; and as I spoke, I experienced His anointing in a totally new and wonderful
way.

After the service, someone drew me aside and said,
"Tonight as you were speaking, the most extraordinary
thing happened. I was looking at you and you suddenly
disappeared. I could hear your voice, but in the pulpit

there was only a brilliant light where you had been standing."

I was grateful for this, but attributed it to a purely subjective experience on this person's part. However, within ten days I received three letters, two of them from clergymen and all of them from "down-to-earth" people, reporting the same phenomenon. I could then only rejoice at His answer to prayer.

"Give thanks for all things" is the scriptural admonition (Eph. 5:20). This must, then, include adversity, which is a challenge enabling us to prove our faith; grief, for it cleanses and throws us completely on the mercy of God, Who binds up the wounds of the broken-hearted (Isa. 61:1); and pain, for God will use it for His glory to alleviate the pain of others. In everything give thanks, adjures Saint Paul. And I know now that this is possible for Christians, for we neither suffer nor sorrow as those who have no hope (I Thess. 4:13).

Hitherto I had given thanks for the way in which God had used my pain, and for the relief of pain, however brief, when it had come. Now, for the first time, I was able to thank Him for the suffering itself; for had I not been in such pain that night of the mission, I doubt that I could have prayed with such wholehearted fervency that He empty me completely of self. There was great healing in this experience; for a short time at least, the climate was as He would have it to be.

To establish the right climate for healing is not easy. To attempt to live one's life in such a climate is even more difficult—but it is a glorious striving, whose goal is God Himself. For in direct proportion to the extent that we are able, by His grace, to relinquish ourselves, to that extent are we able to receive Him who is at once the Light that shineth in our darkness (John 1:5), the source of all joy, of all health and wholeness, and not only the meaning of our life, but life itself.

Chapter 13

LORD,
HEAR OUR PRAYER

ACCORDING TO SAINT TERESA of Avila, "There is but one road which reaches God, and that is prayer."

This is, of course, true, but prayer is not only the road to God. It constitutes the very atmosphere we breathe in the climate of healing; it is the oxygen of the spirit. It is the means by which we establish a relationship with God, and the means through which we are enabled to live continually in that relationship.

As we constantly caution that there is no magic in the sacramental healing rites, so must this caution be extended to prayer, and particularly to healing prayer, for there is no magical formula that inevitably results in healing.

There are many ways of private prayer, and no two people pray in precisely the same way. This is not to say that how we pray is not extremely important; it is. But the importance lies not so much in the words we say as in the attitude behind them. I see a danger, especially in the healing ministry, that because the technique of healing prayer is emphasized, the methodology for some people may supersede the underlying attitude.

For example, we teach that in praying for the sick, we must erase from our minds the symptoms of illness and picture the patient as completely whole. There is great validity in this, but to overemphasize this procedure is to run the risk of thinking that there is some sort of magic involved, that if one's prayer is not accompanied by a vision of the individual as totally well, no healing can possibly result. Although experience indicates that certain kinds of healing prayer are more effective than others, to attempt to stereotype such prayer, to insist that one must pray at all times in exactly the same way, may well lead to superstition.

In praying for healing, we recommend affirmative prayer, not using the escape clause "*If* it be Thy will." Assuming that perfect wholeness *is* God's will, we can pray with assurance; "Thy will be done in him for whom I pray." We suggest offering thanks for the healing even before it is evident; we ask the patient to act, insofar as possible, as if the healing had already taken place. This does not mean stopping medication or throwing away braces. It simply means to adopt an attitude of health, attempting to live a normal life. Insistence upon these methods as invariable and inflexible techniques, however, may carry with it the connotation of magic. In my opinion the elements of prayer we must insist upon as indispensable are those that reflect an attitude of praise and thanksgiving, not only for the healing that has already been begun but also for the privilege of being able to take *everything* to God. "In every thing by prayer and supplication with thanksgiving, let your requests be made known unto God," says Saint Paul (Phil. 4:6).

Scripture tells us that Christ lives to make intercession for us (Heb. 7:25). Thus if we begin our prayers with the supplication "Pray Thyself in me," we cannot go wrong, and there will be no danger of perverting our prayer of the heart into magic incantations of unfelt words.

One of the first requisites of prayer is an inner quiet, a willingness "to be still and know that I am God" (Ps. 46:10). The restlessness of the age in which we live, the frantic running from one religious conference to another, the desire to dwell continuously on the mountain tops of religious experience, are unhealthy. In order truly to pray, it helps to begin by realizing that prayer is not a flamboyant experience to be always ecstatically enjoyed but a quiet relationship with God which is total joy.

The words we say may differ, but there is a general pattern to be followed if we are to pray as Christians. In all prayer, for example, we offer God ourselves. We offer Him our love, praying that He intensify it. We offer Him our faith, praying that He quicken it. We offer Him our commitment, praying that He increase it. We pray that He will cleanse us and use our lives for His glory.

In prayer for healing there is an inevitable tension between battling the evil of sickness and suffering and simultaneously relinquishing ourself, or the one for whom we pray, entirely to God. The value of the words we say lies in the fact that they clarify our thoughts and thus our attitude, an attitude that may be expressed in words something like this: "Take my life, O Lord. Transform it and use it for the blessing [healing] of John Smith."

Believing that it is God's perfect will that we be healed of all brokenness, we know also that the most important healing, and our only real wholeness, lies in offering ourselves to Him that He may fill us with His spirit.

There are many ways of praying for the sick, some of which I have mentioned in another book.[1] Suffice it to say here that among the most simple and effective is that

[1] Emily Gardiner Neal, *Where There's Smoke* (New York: Morehouse-Barlow, 1967), p. 157.

of holding up in the healing light and love of Christ each one for whom we pray. As we take them one by one before the throne of grace, we express our attitude of confidence and trust in those words voiced so long ago: "Lord, behold, he whom thou lovest is sick" (John 11:3). In these words of Martha and Mary, Saint Augustine finds what he terms a model of prayer, teaching us to have immediate recourse to God without waiting until all human means of aid have been exhausted.[2] I myself have found it one of the most powerful of prayers, reflecting our conviction of God's infinite mercy and never-failing compassion.

If we are in doubt, we can never go wrong if we use the prayer our Lord gave us: "Thy will be done on earth as it is in heaven." This one sentence conveys the underlying attitude of all healing prayer as for our entire Christian life.

The story is told of a Franciscan friar of some years ago that everyone he prayed for seemed to recover. Soon people began to come to him from many miles away, as though to a shrine. Again and again his superior asked him about his power, and he invariably replied, "*I* have no power; *I* do nothing. It is God."

Finally the superior learned from him how he prayed.

"I pray only one prayer," the friar said: " 'Thy will be done on earth as it is in heaven.' And I pray it one hundred times each night and morning." Perhaps this is the only prayer any of us would need to pray if we prayed it with all our hearts.

In my experience, the prayer of pure praise also releases exceptional healing power. At least part of the power of this prayer can surely be attributed to the fact that it is entirely selfless.

Many are confused by the distinction made between

---

[2] A Father of the Society of Jesus, *Practical Meditations* (London: Burns and Oates, 1962), p. 717.

praise and thanksgiving. As one woman put it, "You seem to be quibbling over words." No—for while thanksgiving and praise go hand in hand, the difference is not merely a matter of semantics; it lies in a subtle but important difference in attitude. In thanksgiving, as in the other essentials of Christian prayer, all of which are necessary to our total prayer life, there is a strong element of self. In confession, for example, we are thinking of *our* sins; in intercession we are praying for those for whom *we* seek God's blessing; in petition we are asking His help for *our* needs. Likewise, in thanksgiving we are thanking God for something which in some way pleases *us*. However, in the prayer of pure praise, there is no element of self, only simple adoration, and for this reason praise brings us extraordinarily close to God. It might be remarked here that God has not an insatiable craving for our adoration. He needs neither us nor our continual praise. We need *Him*, and the attitude of praise on our parts is for our benefit, and not His.

The well-known novelist Elizabeth Goudge has a priest in one of her books comment that there are three vitally important prayers, each consisting of only three words: "Thee I adore," "Christ have mercy," and "Into Thy hands." Upon these brief prayers we might well build our entire prayer lives, for they convey the attitudes which should lie behind all the prayers we say, in whatever words we choose to use.

During the past few years, much emphasis has been placed on conversational prayer, and rightly so; without such prayer one cannot, in my opinion, be said to truly pray. Yet it is curious that this method of prayer is considered "new," for it has been used for many centuries, as the lives of the great saints of the church attest. Indeed, the classical "textbook" on conversational prayer, Brother Lawrence's *The Practice of the Presence of God*, dates from the seventeenth century.

Typical is the story told of Saint Teresa of Avila, who, when on an unusually arduous journey, complained to God of the difficulties He was placing in her way. When He seemed to reply, "But that is how I treat My friends," the saint answered irritably, "Yes, my Lord, and that is why Thou hast so few of them." [3] This is an amusing and valid example of conversational prayer, in which one talks to God as one feels.

Genuine prayer does not put on pious airs or engage in pietistic rhetoric. We talk to God naturally, telling Him how and what we feel: of our victories and disappointments; of our desires for others and for ourselves; of our gratitude and of our love. Again, this is for *our* benefit, not His. Our talking with Him establishes that personal relationship upon which depends the strength of our prayer life.

Any conversation is a two-way affair, and at least half our prayer time should be spent in listening. Jesus says, "If any man will do His will, he shall know of the doctrine" (John 7:17), which is to say that the insight and knowledge concerning what He taught, the ability to discern the truth that He not only represented but was and is, are given those who do His will.

Many of us fervently desire to be obedient to Him in the specific circumstances in which we find ourselves. The question is, how do we *know* His will in any given situation?

As necessary and good as is Christian vocal prayer, listening prayer is absolutely essential for our spiritual growth, which necessarily includes obedience. For it is only when we listen that we can hear Him speak; and in the noisy activism of the world, that still small voice needs quiet of heart and mind if it is to be heard. With practice we will be able to hear it. Usually the voice

[3] E. Allison Peers, *Mother of Carmel* (London: S.C.M. Press, 1945), p. 136.

comes not as a sound, but as a sense of deep, abiding peace, or a strong, unmistakable impression of what our course of action should be if it is to be according to God's will.

While none of us prays in exactly the same way, I submit one method by which you may learn the art of listening prayer.

First, as in all your prayers, ask that the Holy Spirit pray in you. Say whatever words you wish, but let your attitude be, "Speak, Lord, for thy servant heareth" (I Sam. 3:9). And then be quiet.

I think it useful, especially in the beginning when you are learning to listen, to focus your eyes on something, a cross or a crucifix, or perhaps a picture of Christ. If you close your eyes, it is fatally easy for your thoughts to wander. Even so, from time to time you will find yourself distracted. At these times, draw yourself back by silently repeating the holy name. This is not "vain repetition," for each time you say "Jesus" it is with a different emphasis: "I worship You"; "Have mercy"; "Forgive"; "Open my ears that I may hear Your voice." Speak the holy name slowly, with long intervals of silence in between. It is in these times of silence that you will finally hear.

In so praying, you may be led into contemplation, to which one comes by the prayer of simplicity and quiet. The word "contemplation" need not frighten you. It means in essence and in its simplest form just being with God in love; your mind, your lips, and even your heart stilled, your spirit fixed on God. This type of prayer is not for a favored few living the enclosed life, It is, as the Archbishop of Canterbury writes, "accessible to any man, woman or child who is ready to try to be obedient and humble, and to want God very much." [4] As the Archbishop

[4] Arthur Michael Ramsey, *Sacred and Secular* (New York: Harper and Row, 1965), p. 45.

goes on to say, "Contemplative prayer is the prayer of hunger and thirst, of desire for God—such is the prayer which links Christianity and ordinary life." [5]

No matter how you choose to go about it, it is necessary, if you would be obedient, not only to scan Scripture seeking to obey the injunctions of our Lord found there, but to search the mind of Christ, which can be done only by the spirit of God within you. It is He who reveals that which we must know in order to be truly obedient, and in our obedience, enabled by grace to comprehend, however inadequately, God's revelation of Himself; to have, by the action of the Holy Spirit, God's will illumined for us.

The goal of the Christian is to live in a state of habitual prayer, to which we come by practicing the presence of God.

This we may do in a number of ways, no matter how busy we may be with other things. Brief words of praise may be offered throughout the day (as mentioned in Chapter 10); a "for Thy glory, Lord" spoken before each task we do; the frequent repetition of the holy name—any method you wish that will keep you aware of God.

The time will come, no matter how occupied our conscious minds, when our subconscious will be continually aware of Him. It will become a natural instinct and not a self-conscious effort to pray for those we pass on the street who look harassed or unhappy; to offer prayer as an ambulance clangs by or we pass a funeral procession.

Instinctively we will pray for the disagreeable taxi driver, and suddenly he smiles and begins to talk—and we know why. Instinctively we pray for the cross clerk in a store, and suddenly she becomes pleasant and cooperative. These are small miracles of prayer, but miracles they are. Countless people whom we shall never

[5] *Ibid.*, p. 58.

know may well be touched and blessed by our prayers in passing.

As Christians, we are called to pray for our enemies. I still remember the shock and indignation of some, when at the healing service at Calvary immediately following the assassination of Robert Kennedy, I offered prayer not only for the Kennedy family but for the assassin. "Bless them that curse you, and pray for them which despitefully use you, and persecute you" (Matt. 5:44) is His command.

Thus we pray as well for those we simply may not like. In our prayers we *will* them all the best; we *will* to love them, and often the time comes when we, through God, can even like them!

Our prayer life is not complete unless we set aside definite times for prayer, at least at night and in the morning. Some time ago, a woman who is under my spiritual direction demurred at the thought of any formal prayer time.

"I pray throughout the day," she said, "when I'm cleaning or washing the dishes or making the beds. Why then must I pray also at set times?"

Simply because there should be occasions when we go before the throne of almighty God giving Him our complete and undivided attention, the only thought on our minds Him whom we worship. We attempt to follow the example of our Lord, who, although His whole life was a prayer, yet withdrew again and again to pray.

If we practice the presence of God throughout the day, and if we draw apart, however briefly, at certain set intervals, prayer can become for us a way of life. Busy young parents can achieve this life as well as any monastic, and I know many who do.

It has been observed that many people, concerned solely with personal salvation, do not have a real sense of what the Body of Christ—of which we are all members and Christ the Head—really is. The importance of the corporate nature of the Body often seems to be underestimated.

Participating together in the worship of the church, we link our prayers with the faithful, with "angels and archangels and all the company of heaven" (B.C.P., p. 77). We are an indispensable part of a holy fellowship, spiritually one with all Christians, living and dead. To the extent that we fail to participate in corporate worship, to that extent do we weaken the Body.

There are many great liturgical prayers that we can make our own. These may help us develop in the life of prayer, so that we may outgrow the kindergarten prayers and attitudes of our childhood.

It behooves us to learn all we can about prayer, although we can never learn it all. Yet I think we must guard against becoming enmeshed in techniques. No "computerized" type of prayer, no matter how eloquent the words, can equal the silent lifting of the heart to God. I believe that no prayer, however inadequate (and all prayer is in some sense inadequate), goes unheard by Him—for it is as someone has said: "When a little girl prays for her rag doll, the whole world benefits." [6]

[6] *The Living Church,* Nov. 22, 1970, p. 2.

Chapter 14

DEPRESSION AND GUILT

SINCE I HAVE BEEN ASSOCIATED with the healing ministry, I have been confronted with an increasing number of cases of depression. These range from recurring bouts of feeling "down" to that deep depression which is devastating and in large part incapacitating.

Some cases of profound, long-lasting depression have been healed instantly by the power of God. Still more have been healed in a relatively short time by spiritual counseling and regular attendance at healing services. Others require the help of a psychologist or psychiatrist as well as healing prayer. If you are among the last, it is nothing to be ashamed of, any more than you should be ashamed of seeking medical help for a case of pneumonia. Both are illnesses, and if you require psychotherapy it does not denote a lack of faith. God can indeed heal all things. His power is always there for you to receive, but sometimes the very nature of your illness prevents your receiving it. Your heart is temporarily locked shut by the key of fear, which is symptomatic of emotional disturbance. A combination of prayer and psychiatric help will alleviate your fear, and as your tension lessens, your heart will open so that you may receive the healing grace God is so eager to bestow upon you.

To be forewarned is to be forearmed, and it is well to remember that if physical illness tends to be accompanied by guilt feelings, these feelings are often intensified in cases of depression. We think that as Christians who know and believe the incredibly good news of the gospel, we should never feel "down," but instead continually manifest in our lives the joy of the Lord. So we should, when we are well; but sometimes we cannot when we are emotionally disturbed. It is a curious paradox that the Christian, who of all people knows the source of all forgiveness, should at the same time suffer so greatly from feelings of guilt. This must continually break the heart of God, for it actually negates our Lord's sacrifice on the cross for our sins.

Not long ago I received a letter from a clergyman who lives far from Pittsburgh. It was a heartbreaking letter, telling me of his battle against a depression from which he could not extricate himself and which had completely incapacitated him as far as his work was concerned. Adding to the difficulty of the entire situation was the fact that his teen-age children were disillusioned and their faith seriously undermined.

"How," they asked "could it be possible that their father, a dedicated Christian minister, could be so afflicted?" Such questioning in the face of illness, disaster, or death is the reason I so continually emphasize that Christianity is not a passport into a utopian land of no disease, no trouble of any kind. What *is* unique to the Christian is his knowledge that the trials and tribulations of this world have no dominion over him, that the promise "He will not fail thee nor forsake thee" (Deut. 31:6) is a valid one, that in this knowledge lies the Christian's strength and consolation.

The guilt feelings from which this pastor suffered were

insupportable, obviously intensified in him because of his calling. By his letter it was abundantly clear that this minister was seriously ill emotionally and should be receiving psychiatric help. However, on the spiritual side, I felt I could justifiably offer the counsel he sought. He was, for example, in such a state of despair that he was convinced that he was no longer within the providence of God. I could assure him, because I was so sure, that he was *not* outside God's grace, and that his only real sin lay in thinking his sins so great and his faith so small that God would not and could not forgive him.

I recalled to this tortured man, and asked him to claim, the scriptural promise: "If we confess our sins, He is faithful and just to forgive us our sins and to cleanse us from all unrighteousness" (I John 1:9). Then I suggested that he offer his doubts, his sins and his depression, to God. I related to him a story of which I am very fond, which is applicable not only to the distraught clergyman of whom I speak but also to every single one of us.

It concerns the desert father who offered to God his life of hardship, but God rejected it. Then the saint offered all his work in his translation of Holy Scripture—but God rejected this. Finally, in desperation, the desert father cried, "But Lord, I have offered You all I have. What then do You want?"

Loud and clear came the answer: "I want your sins, my son."

Our sins, our fears and doubts, are part of us. Our self-offering is not complete unless we also offer these. God wants all of us, *especially* our sins, that He may have the joy of forgiving.

For innumerable people, the prayer for the healing of the memories described by Agnes Sanford [1] and now

---

[1] Agnes Sanford, *Healing Gifts of the Spirit* (Philadelphia: J. B. Lippincott, 1966), p. 125.

used by many has proved extraordinarily effective. In brief, this prayer consists of taking the person in need to Jesus and asking Him to walk back through time, beginning with the person's infancy and continuing up to the present. Adapted to individual circumstances, my abbreviated version goes something like this: "Jesus, please go back in time to when this individual was a tiny baby crying for his bottle and feeling forsaken. Hold him in Your arms, Lord, and comfort him. Now please go to the bedside of this five-year-old child, who lies in his nursery afraid of the dark. Reach out Your hand, Lord, and comfort him, that he will not be afraid. Now please go to that ten-year-old who feels himself unjustly punished and rejected. Hold him, Lord, that he may know how greatly he is loved."

We continue in this vein through adolescence up to the present, asking at each stage of the patient's life that God will cleanse and forgive. We pray for the complete healing of all those early memories and impressions, offering thanksgiving at each stage, and ask that he be enabled by grace to receive the fullness of God's mercy and forgiveness won for us on Calvary.

A deeply devout woman who was suffering from depression used this prayer and, like so many, was delivered from her disturbance. At this writing there has been no recurrence for four years. She made one visit to her psychiatrist to present herself as healed. When she told him of this type of prayer, he was intensely interested, considered it excellent therapy, and asked her for a copy.

Some months ago a man wrote me from another state telling me that he was flying to Calvary for the healing service the following week. He asked to talk with me a few minutes before the service. The gentleman was suffering from deep depression and unable to work. Midway during our interview, he remarked that he was a physician, but had come to Calvary not as a doctor but as a Christian. When it was time to go in to the service, I asked him what his medical specialty was, and he replied that he was a psychiatrist.

At the healing service he came to me for the laying on of hands, and I prayed very briefly for the healing of the memories. After the service we met, and he told me of an extraordinary happening which had occurred at the altar rail. He said that as he received the laying on of hands with prayer, there suddenly flooded to the surface of his mind memories of anger, hostility, and feelings of rejection that he had undergone as a child; he had never known until that moment that they existed in his unconscious mind. As Jesus walked back through time in the life of this man, each hurt had been healed. A letter from him shortly thereafter told me he was back at work full time—a new creature in Christ.

If you are suffering from an inexplicable depression, you may well find this type of prayer beneficial. Ask someone to pray it for you, or pray it for yourself.

As depression is complicated by feelings of guilt, so can guilt lead to and increase depression. My personal observation leads me to conclude that generally speaking, people fall into three categories in their response to guilt.

First, there are those with strong guilt feelings who seek to deny their guilt, when actually there may be good reason for it. Real guilt cannot be stifled without deleterious consequences. A visit to Bellevue Hospital in New York made it clear that such guilt must be removed before the sick person can recover. This is why the cooperation of psychiatrist and clergyman is vitally important in the treatment of those who need to know the forgiveness of God before they can be successfully treated medically. In some cases, the ability to accept His forgiveness is of itself sufficent "treatment."

In this connection I recall a woman suffering from deep

depression deriving from guilt occasioned by a love affair in which she had engaged several years before she was married. Her psychiatrist had urged her to tell her husband of the affair, but before doing so, she consulted me. While trying never to interfere with the work of a psychiatrist, in this case I felt obliged to say that I thought this would be a great mistake; that she might well jeopardize her marriage, and that by the hurt inflicted thus upon her husband, her own sense of guilt would, in my opinion, be increased rather than diminished.

I remember how the despair in her eyes turned to hope, as with all the authority at my command, I assured her of the forgiveness of God. I recall how the hope in her eyes turned to joy, as holding her hands in mine, she repeated after me, "Jesus, I accept your forgiveness according to Your promise. Thank You." By so simple an act, that woman's burden of guilt lifted, and with it the depression, and her life was transformed.

In the second category of guilt are Christians who are overscrupulous in regard to their own soul-searching for possible and often nonexistent sins.

Scrupulosity is one of the bugbears many of us have to face as we grow in the spiritual life; for as we grow, we become increasingly aware of our own sin, which in the presence of the utter holiness of God appalls us. Up to a point, this is as it should be, for "He who says he is without sin deceives himself; and there is no truth in him" (I John 1:8). However, if we focus our attention exclusively on our sin instead of Christ, forgetting the mercy of God, if we attribute to ourselves sins of which we are not guilty, and agonize over sins of which we know we are, we become neurotically introverted. We have forgotten that while Saint John tells us that there is no truth in us if we say we are without sin, so does he tell us, in the very next verse, that "God is faithful and just to forgive us our sins." If we fail to progress to this latter pronouncement and do not accept the assurance of God's forgiveness, we do violence to the Christian faith.

In the third category of guilt are those who, if they have not committed an overt act, such as robbing a bank, honestly do not know what sin is; yet they feel guilty. Perhaps it is as some theologians have conjectured, that the guilt feelings which plague so many, Christians or not, stem from original sin.

There are various sins of the spirit of which most of us are guilty, at least from time to time—sins which wreak havoc in our lives. Here I want to mention specifically anger, because there is so much confusion about this emotion. Time and again I am asked if anger is ever justified. I believe that it is, and my belief is scripturally founded. But we must constantly beware of holding anger in hate, and attempting to justify such anger as "righteous indignation." To be angry in hate is obviously a sin; but there can be anger *without* sin, if on the other side of the coin is love.

Paul says, "Be angry and sin not" (Eph. 4:26). The Phillips translation reads, "Be sure your anger is not out of wounded pride or bad temper." Thus the source of our anger must be our guideline.

We recall the life of our Lord. He was a far cry from the namby-pamby, sentimental "sweet Jesus" of the old Sunday School books. Rather was He a virile man of power. He was gentle, yes, for gentleness and strength go hand in hand; it is only the strong who dare to be gentle.

Our Lord certainly manifested anger, but it was a holy anger, springing from love and concern. He drove out the money changers in the Temple (Matt. 21:12); "Ye generation of vipers," He exclaimed to the Pharisees (Matt. 12:34); and in no uncertain terms He hurled at them the words, "Woe unto you, scribes and Pharisees, hypocrites!" (Matt. 23:13). And when His disciples failed to heal the lunatic child, his response was "O faithless and perverse generation! How long shall I be with you? How long shall I suffer you!" (Matt. 17:17).

Such words surely denote anger. Nevertheless, His anger was always the other side of the coin of love. As we strive to follow in His footsteps, we, too, must realize that were it not for anger (*not* bad temper), were it not for righteous indignation, nothing constructive would ever be accomplished in the world, no injustice ever rectified, no bad laws ever changed to good.

The opposite of righteous indignation may well be indifference—for indifference, not anger, is to me the sin of the world. It is indifference, not atheism, that is the arch enemy of the Christian faith; and where there is indifference, there is no concern for minority groups, for the poor, for all who suffer.

"Be angry and sin not." But let us be angry over situations and not at people. This is another way of saying, "Be angry over—and hate—the sin, but never the sinner."

Chapter 15

ARE YOU ANXIOUS OR AFRAID?

FEW OF US in these troubled times are totally immune from anxiety. Our anxieties, like our depressions, range from being merely troublesome to complete incapacitation. The answer to a life shackled by anxiety and bound by fear is faith in the Lord Jesus, for in Christ is found the answer to all things. If He were the supreme reality in our lives, if we could keep our eyes always and entirely focused on Him alone, we would keep out of trouble. Our faith would then be the power it is meant to be: not of *itself* the power to save and to heal, but the means by which we come to wholly accept Him who does both.

When we take our eyes off Christ we sink, as did Peter when he walked on the water. For just a second the disciple took His eyes off Jesus; fear immediately overcame him, and he went down (Matt. 14:30). So it is with us when the circumstances of our lives, our anxieties, frustrations, and fears, assume priority over our Lord. When they and not He become for us the great reality, we sink, drowning in their morass.

Actually, anxiety is the negation of the Spirit of God in us, for love, which *is* God, casts out fear (I John 4:18). If we loved enough or believed sufficiently in His love for us, none of us would be anxious or afraid.

I do not refer to that pathological anxiety state which is an illness. But, to the extent that the patient is able to absorb them, the same truths apply as to the "garden variety" under discussion here. For much of all anxiety derives from the past, and much is concerned with things to come. The ultimate result is that many of us have virtually no present at all.

The moment we are disobedient to God, the instant that we break a spiritual law, we suffer the consequences—which are self-induced and not God-produced. We might remember that the thrust of Christ's teaching in this regard is to live in the present, one day at a time. "Do not be anxious about tomorrow," He enjoins us. "Tomorrow will look after itself" (Matt. 6:34 N.E.B.).

Although some may live in the past and others only for the future, the Christian, in obedience to his Lord, should live in the present. He should be informed by the past, yes, but not agonized over what has been done or left undone; expectant of the future, yes, but never apprehensive over what in all probability will never come to pass. To live other than in this way—to sacrifice our present on the altar of a past filled with remorse and a future dimmed by fear—is to waste our lives.

A woman came to me in devastating remorse over the mistakes she had made in the past, beginning with her marriage some ten years before, when she had married her husband on the rebound. As a result, early in her marriage, she had taken out on her husband her unhappiness and her longing for the other man. She had two children, to whom she realized she had been a nervous and highly irritable mother.

To add to her difficulties, she had engaged in an extramarital affair several years after her marriage. By the time she came to me she was in a pitiable state, unable to sleep, guilt-ridden and thoroughly miserable—for by now she had come to love and appreciate her husband. They could have had a happy life together, but she was so racked by regret over her past that she had neither present nor future.

She had forgotten the love and forgiveness of God. It took her approximately three months of weekly counseling to be able to accept His forgiveness and realize His absolution. At last, knowing herself cleansed and restored, she was able for the first time in ten years to live happily in the present.

Less dramatic and perhaps more frequent are cases such as that of a man who was tormenting himself because some years before he had made what proved to be an unwise business decision. He had been offered an opportunity to go with a then-new company. With a wife and three children, he had been afraid at the time to sacrifice his security for the unknown quantity of a new enterprise. The years went on. He had security but with a comparatively small salary.

The company that he had not dared join had thrived, and it was clear that had he not been afraid he would now be a wealthy man. But to all who make what appear later to be wrong decisions, whether in our business or personal lives, I would say as I did to him, "You did what seemed best to you at the time. It is done and over with. So forget it."

As for our fear of the future, most often what we fear does not come to pass. I think of a man I know who at the age of fifty-three had been let go by his company through no fault of his own. He eventually found another job, well paying but with no pension. This man had no present because he was so worried about the future.

"What will my wife and I do when I am forced to retire?" he asked in near panic. "Social Security certainly won't take care of us."

During the time that he was counseling with me, he received an unexpected inheritance from a distant relative. This, coupled with a reasonable savings plan, would enable him and his wife to live comfortably after his retirement, even if not in the style to which they had been accustomed. So his worry about the future had been in vain; in vain, that is, until he came to understand that our Lord never promised His followers cake—only bread—but the Bread of Life.

In this connection we recall again the prayer that Jesus taught us, "Give us day by day our daily bread" (Luke 11:3). There is no implication here that we should ever pray, "Give us cake and caviar and Cadillacs for the rest of our lives."

God gave us the brains we have, and He intends us to use them. In adjuring us not to worry about tomorrow, He does not mean us to do what a fanatic of my acquaintance did. This was a man with five children who interpreted our Lord's words to mean, "Don't prepare for the future." As a result, he canceled his life insurance policies. Shortly thereafter he was killed in an accident, leaving his family destitute.

This sort of irresponsibility is not what our Lord meant. He said, "Don't worry." He never said, "Don't prepare; don't carry life insurance; don't save for a rainy day."

So many of us waste half our strength in panicky anticipation of unpleasant things to come and the other half in continuing remorse over a past already gone that we have no strength left for the present. To live in this way is proof positive of our lack of trust in God.

Some chronic worriers have said to me, "You don't take into account temperamental differences. Some people are just born worriers."

Those who say this are correct: I do *not* take into account temperamental differences in this area of life. I know only too well that some people are born worriers, because I was one. If there was not something to worry about, I'd manage to manufacture something, and worry myself into a state of near collapse. But I have learned that if one is a Christian one need not remain a "born" worrier. I have learned that the best way on earth to wreck one's life is to try to take it into one's own hands, thrusting aside the hand of God, which is always there to bless, to heal, and to guide us. But we must grasp that hand when He extends it to us.

I offer here two practical suggestions. First, if you are suffering from anxiety, share your apprehension with only one person—someone you can trust. To broadcast your worries far and wide only magnifies them.

Second, practice living in what the French theologian J. P. de Caussade calls the "Sacrament of the present moment." [1] This is a difficult concept, which will take time to put into effect, but keep trying, for it is well worth the effort.

In brief, the idea consists of abandoning yourself to the will of God, moment by moment. Do not worry about His will either in retrospect or in advance; just try to live in the serenity of God's present intention for you. Center your attention on God's grace and will as they bear upon you instant by instant. Once you are centered in the present moment (neither in the past nor the future), this continuing act or surrender to Him becomes a simple, joyous, and infinitely wonderful thing. It "works," as I know from personal experience. This does not mean that in your life there will never be trouble or anxiety or tension; but it does mean that these things will be caught up in the flood of God's love and mercy, moment by moment.

[1] J. P. de Caussade, S.J., *Self Abandonment to Divine Providence* (London: Burns, Oates and Washbourne Ltd., 1959).

Anyone can learn to enter the present moment and surrender. Ask God what He wants of you now (not tomorrow or next week). Ask the Holy Spirit to open your spiritual ears so that you may hear what He is telling you.

As you gradually learn to abandon yourself to His will and plan for you, instant by instant, your remorse over the past will lessen and your worry over the future will diminish. Unimpeded by either past or future, you will find yourself living in the fullness of life in the present, and you will experience in a new way the peace of God—or, more accurately, peace *with* God.

Our Lord said, "My peace I give unto you (John 14:27). He spoke these words shortly before His betrayal and crucifixion, which He knew were shortly to occur. He spoke them to His apostles, whom He knew, as He said, "the world will hate" (John 15:19). He knew the hardship, the conflicts, the persecution which they would endure for His sake; and yet He said, "My peace I give unto you."

This is the peace which is not of this world and which has little to do with it. It is a peace that exists in your heart regardless of what has happened in the past or what may happen in the future. It is peace of mind, but far more than that. It is an ineffable peace of the heart and spirit, which comes from knowing God and striving to live according to His will. It is a peace that, regardless of trial and tribulation, lies at the core of our being, and cannot be disturbed no matter what happens to us outwardly. It is the peace that can be found only in our certain knowledge that He lives, that He dwells in us and we in Him. And so long as this is true, there is no room within us to harbor undue anxiety or fear.

As John the Baptist said, "He must increase, but I must decrease" (John 3:30). In direct proportion to His increase in our lives do we experience His peace. The key to the peace of God, as to all healing and the entire Chris-

tian life, is "Seek ye the kingdom of God" (Luke 12:31).
However, so often we believe that we *are* seeking first
the kingdom, that we *are* putting Christ first, when in
truth we are not.

In this connection I think of a devout Christian who
came to me suffering from hypertension. He appeared
nervous, and voiced extreme apprehension concerning his
job, an apprehension not for himself but for his wife. He
was fearful of being passed over for a promotion, and his
wife badly wanted the extra money this would bring. A
little sharp practice on his part, not actually cheating,
and the promotion would almost certainly be his. The
difficulty was that he was in a state of conflict, waging a
battle with his conscience.

When he asked my advice, I could only urge him to
obey his conscience, for it seemed clear to me that this
was God speaking to him. Sensing the type of person
he was, I knew that he must put God first in his life if he
were to know peace of heart. As it was, he was trying to
put his wife ahead of Christ.

I recalled to him how at the age of twelve Jesus had
lingered in the temple, badly worrying his parents, who
thought Him lost. He loved them deeply, but when His
mother chastised Him, He had to reply, "Wist ye not that
I must be about my Father's business?" (Luke 2:49).

"But I love my wife," the man said to me. Of course,
and so did Jesus love His family—but the Father had to
come first, and so it is with us.

I well knew what it would do to this man's personal
integrity were he to do what he planned to achieve the
promotion for his wife's sake. His action would destroy
not only him but also the relationship with his wife he
was so anxious to preserve. Guilt-ridden, he would never
again know God's peace, and subconsciously he would
hold his wife responsible.

I extracted a promise from the man that he would do

nothing whatsoever to further his promotion for a period of six weeks. During this time he was to pray the situation through.

Within three weeks, he called to tell me that he had been given the job he wanted without his having to make a move. As an aside, he remarked that his blood pressure was normal, which news came as no surprise.

It is just as Jesus told us: Only when we are willing to lose our life (and this includes our job and everything else we may think important) for His sake are we able to find it (Luke 9:24); and in the finding we experience that peace of God without which we cannot be truly whole.

Our Lord never promised us freedom from hardship, but He gave us Himself and His transfiguring power. He never promised that we would not have to suffer, but He gave His assurance that He would be always with us. It is through the healing ministry, where there seems such an intense awareness of His presence, that we are uniquely enabled to realize the sufficiency of this promise. It is at the altars of His healing church that we most often dare to claim it.

As we cannot receive Christ unless we first give Him ourselves, without qualification or reservation, neither can we fully experience His love for us until we give it back to Him.

"The measure you give," He says, "will be the measure you get, and still more will be given you" (Mark 4:24 R.S.V.). And the greater the intensity of our love for Him, the more of His love we are enabled to receive and then return to Him. It is a continuous cycle of giving and receiving, each time marvelously more, until at last we truly abide in Him, and *know* that He abides in us. With this inner knowing comes that peace which the world can neither give nor take away.

As our hearts come at last to rest in the knowledge that

"the eternal God is thy refuge, and underneath are the everlasting arms" (Deut. 33:27), we are able to live more nearly as He would have us to live, without anxiety or fear. We can live in the present, moment by moment, striving to know and do His will, looking neither behind with regret nor ahead with trepidation.

It is through Scripture, sacrament and prayer, through penitence and adoration, that we finally come to know Him whom we worship. Then it is that the kingdom of God becomes for us a present reality as well as a future hope. We know at last the meaning of His words, and take them to ourselves: "My peace I give unto you."

Chapter 16

GOD LOVES *YOU*

LONELINESS SEEMS TO BE one of humanity's most prevalent ailments. I consider it an "ailment" because at the least it can cause great misery for those who suffer from it, and at the most, if untended, it can lead to a deep, pathological depression.

Some time ago I took a course in which mankind's basic needs were under discussion. At the head of the list on the blackboard, the instructor had written in large white letters the word "acceptance," a popular word today, with which I take exception when used in such a context. I am convinced that it is not merely acceptance but *love* that human beings require.

In my opinion to receive love and to give love are basic needs. As Christians we can and should help those who are lonely by giving them of ourselves and our time. We can and should help those who feel themselves unloved by loving them (and letting them know it), whoever and wherever they may be.

About a year ago, a young man brought to Christ through the Calvary ministry, on fire with zeal, was transferred by his company from Pittsburgh to another city. He was a new Christian of only a few months, and during

132

these months he had regularly attended the healing
services and been deeply involved with a prayer group.
Thus he had been well nurtured by his new-found Christian friends.

The day before he left Pittsburgh I talked with him
and cautioned him not to be discouraged in his new
environment, where he might have difficulty in finding
people of like mind and spirit. As we are all aware, there
is not a superabundance of committed Christians, and
when we are moved to a new location, it usually takes a
while to ferret them out.

I warned him against the frustration he would feel
when he wanted to shout from the rooftops, "Christ
lives"—and no one would listen. And I warned him
against loneliness. At this he demurred. "Surely no one
who knows Christ can ever be lonely," he said.

In one sense he was of course correct. The loneliness of
the Christian is very different from that of the pagan. It is,
in fact, a glorious thing—but nevertheless, it *is* loneliness.

Some weeks later I received a letter from this young
man, telling me that he was suffering from the sense of
keen frustration I had foreseen. Furthermore, he was
desperately lonely, even though he knew Christ. He had
not been a Christian long enough to realize the cost of the
faith, and one of its costs is loneliness.

Humanly speaking, the life of the spirit is an intensely
lonely one. At the core of every individual's being is an
area that no other person, no matter how intimate or devoted—not even a husband or wife—can penetrate. It is
an inviolable loneliness. This is true of everyone, Christian or otherwise, but it is especially true of the Christian,
for Christians are *in* the world but not *of* it, and there is a
constant tension involved in having one foot in heaven
and the other on earth. Yet though loneliness can be a
curse for the unbeliever, for the Christian it is—or can be
—a blessed state, because it enables us to share in the

loneliness of the Lord Jesus as He walked the earth. The "Son of Man hath not where to lay his head" (Matt. 8:20), and his disciples have always been "strangers and pilgrims on the earth" (Heb. 11:13).

But if we offer our loneliness to Christ, we are brought ever closer to the God we worship. Loneliness is part of the cross we are called upon, and deeply privileged, to carry. When we carry it in His name and for His sake, the yoke is easy and the burden light (Matt. 11:30).

Loneliness is thus a blessed state, but paradoxically it is our holy obligation to mitigate it whenever we find it in others, whether they be Christians or not, and to relieve it by the love of God manifested through us.

One evidence of loneliness is the crying need of so many to have someone to talk to, and to *listen*. I remember a winter night when my telephone rang about midnight. The call was from a distraught woman, saying she was all alone, ill, and contemplating suicide. She asked that I go to her at once.

I was in bed, it was a bad night, the roads covered with snow and ice, and the woman lived about as far from me as possible and still be in Pittsburgh. I was not overly enthusiastic at the prospect of crawling out of my warm bed and braving the elements, but sensing the urgency in her voice, I was afraid to delay my visit until morning.

When I reached my destination, I was greeted by an elderly woman, her face strained and white with evidence of recent tears. As she talked, I learned that her husband had died the year before; but it was soon evident that she had no intention of taking her life, nor was she physically ill.

My initial reaction was one of some annoyance that she had lied to me over the telephone. However, as she talked I realized that she did indeed suffer from a sickness: an intolerable loneliness, which had reached its climax at that hour, and which required alleviation as surely as any agonizing physical pain. She had stood it as long as she was able, and then her need to talk, to know that someone cared, overpowered her.

I stayed with her for nearly two hours, and it was time well spent, for I left her serene, knowing that someone was concerned. Obviously one cannot place oneself at the perpetual disposal of neurotics who make unreasonable demands. Such was not the case with this particular woman, who was, I learned later, a considerate and honest person. It was simply that on this one night her need was so overwhelming that it transcended every other consideration.

In the vast majority of cases, an occasional visit during the day to someone who needs to talk and be listened to, who needs the assurance of someone's genuine concern, can make the difference between a life of tenable contentment or one of veritable hell. To visit the lonely is such a small act of Christian service that one wishes more people would perform it and thus assist in alleviating a tiny fraction of the world's anguish.

In regard to loneliness among Christians, we see yet another paradox. The more we know of God, the more we long to know, for in direct proportion to our growing knowledge of Him is our holy desire for more and more of Him. This desire never abates as long as we live; curiously enough, as we grow in the knowledge and love of God, as we grow in the life of the spirit, so does a nostalgia, a certain kind of loneliness, increase. This is in actuality a blessing bestowed by God, for it makes us to an ever greater degree dependent upon Christ, Who is our fulfillment, and in Whom there is no aloneness at all.

Our very loneliness is part of the faith we embrace, and it paves the way to holiness. It is given real and deep meaning as it involves us increasingly more in Christ and continually throws us on His mercy and not that of other people; for it is God and God alone Whose mercy never fails us.

It is through Him that we come eventually to recognize

the difference between loneliness and aloneness, for these two words are by no means synonymous. But the remedy for both is the same: to love. And to love is also part of the cost of the faith we embrace. To love is to make oneself vulnerable to what can seem almost unbearable hurts: the love of a wife for her husband who is having an affair with another woman; the love of parents for their children who may get into serious trouble or later on neglect them; the love of friends who may let one down.

As Louis Evely asserts, "To love a person means inevitably to depend on him, it means giving him power over us. By loving us of His own free will, God has chosen to give us power over Him." [1]

Thus even God Himself is vulnerable, because He loves.

The way to help others in their loneliness is by your love. But I would go further and say that if you have never known loneliness within yourself, you cannot offer love, for you cannot feel or know—and therefore cannot meet—the deep need of the truly lonely.

"Whosoever he be of you that forsaketh not all that he hath, he cannot be my disciple," Jesus said (Luke 14:33).

This is a basic premise of the religious life as it is lived in community, but it applies equally to those of us who live in the world. This does not mean that you should neglect your family or abandon your friends or that you should love your family and friends less. It simply means that you must love God more in order to more truly love them. And as you love Him more, His grace is in your heart to minister His love to the lonely. As you come to learn your total dependence upon Him, His grace is in your eyes to minister His joy to the de-

[1] Louis Evely, *We Dare to Say Our Father* (New York: Herder and Herder, 1965), p. 45.

spairing. As you live increasingly in and for Him, His
grace is on your lips to minister His peace. For again,
paradoxically, while the life of the spirit is in a sense
a lonely one, you possess that glorious knowledge, of
heart and mind and spirit, that in and with Him there
can be no real *aloneness* at all.

"And the Lord God said, It is not good that man
should be alone" (Gen. 2:18). Unless we are called to
live the life of a desert hermit, which is not likely in this
day and age, we should be able to depend at least to
some extent upon our fellow human beings to alleviate
the human loneliness that is the lot of many who are
alone in the world. If you are a Christian, you will know
yourself bound to your fellow Christians in the strongest
of bonds—that of the Holy Spirit, by Whom all Christians
are made one in Christ. But however true this is, and
however effectively your association with other Christians
may mitigate your loneliness, what about the aloneness from which you may suffer and which no one can
relieve, if you do not know in your heart the reality of the
love of God?

We hear the words "the love of God" so often without
really knowing what they mean that this phrase has
become for many of us merely a pious cliché. It was so
with me long after I had become a Christian, until that
never-to-be-forgotten day when I first experienced the
supranatural love of God as I laid hands on a man suffering from a critical heart ailment. In the middle of the
healing prayer there was such an awareness of the presence of Christ and His overwhelming love that I could
not continue the vocal prayer. His love flooded the room.
After kneeling by the sick man's bed and offering thanksgiving, he turned to me with a look of extraordinary radiance, and said, "Today I have known God." And so
had I.

Many people claim that we can know the love of God

only as it is manifested through other human beings. This is only half true: We can experience His love directly in circumstances such as I have just described, and which since then have been repeated countless times both for me and for many.

So often people say to me, "How can *I* experience the love of God of which you speak?" First, every healing service in which I participate seeks, through God, to give this experience to those who attend: To know the love of Christ in this way is in reality to experience God Himself, who *is* love. And this, as far as I am concerned, is the primary purpose of the healing ministry. Second, the full answer to this question can be given only by the Holy Spirit Himself. It is because His presence is so peculiarly intensified at healing services that I urge people to attend on a regular basis. The average person gradually grows in receptivity, until at last he is able to receive that which God is so eager to give, namely, Himself—and with Himself comes that abundant life promised by our Lord (John 10:10).

Sometimes the reality of the love of God comes to us during prayer as a sudden revelation, but most often it is a gradual process, a slow and sometimes painful opening of our hearts and understanding by the Holy Spirit, who, if we will only permit Him, stands ready to lead us unerringly into all truth—the love of God and the kingdom disclosed by Jesus. We are far from understanding *how,* but we know a little of *what* is necessary on our part if we are to experience God. One thing of which we are sure is that if we love God only when things go well, only for the material happiness He has given us, only for the healing He proffers us in the name of Jesus, we are not really loving God at all; we are loving only His gifts. We truly love God only when we can say with Saint Ignatius, "Give me only Thy love and Thy grace. With Thee I am rich enough nor do I ask for aught besides."

We must believe with our hearts that "God so loved the world, that He gave His only begotten Son" (John 3:16). These words are so familiar that they tend to fall on deaf ears. What, actually, do they mean to you?

They mean that the Son of God gave Himself not for an impersonal world, a faceless mass of humanity, but for *you*. It is as Saint Paul says: "The Son of God who loved me, and gave himself for me" (Gal. 2:20).

He knows each of His sheep by name, and this means *you*. He knows and cares about *you* so much that He knows the number of hairs on your head (Matt. 10:30). When He says, "Come unto me" (Matt. 11:28), He is calling *you*.

Once your heart can truly perceive the fact that God loves *you* in the most profound and personal way, your battle against aloneness is half won. Total victory lies in your response to His love, thus fulfilling your need to love as well as to be loved.

"We love him, because he first loved us" (I John 4:19). Now at last you have empirical knowledge of this statement. You finally know in your innermost being that God loves *you* and not just "us." You are then able to respond emotionally to His love, thus setting in motion the whole process of the love of God, the mystical exchange of His love for us and ours for Him.

"We have known and believed the love that God hath to us. God is love; and he that dwelleth in love dwelleth in God and God in him" (I John 4:16). In this mutual abiding lies an everlasting divine companionship and the end forever of our aloneness.

Chapter 17

THE BODY OF CHRIST

THE STATE OF MOST CHURCHES today ranges from confusion to chaos. The decline in church attendance is attributed to the fact that the church is not relevant to this age—a charge that is being met alternately or simultaneously by an often extreme liberalism, exaggerated social activism, and changes of liturgy that seek to update and modernize our worship. Notwithstanding all these efforts, millions are turning to the occult. Surely this is saying something that the church is failing to hear.

The charge that the established church is obsolete and not geared to meet the needs of this sophisticated and scientifically oriented era seems curious as we observe the practices that great masses of people now consider "relevant" to their needs: astrology, spiritualism, and witchcraft, all of which predate Christianity by thousands of years. The name of Sybil Leek, present-day "good" witch and high priestess of the occult, is as well known to millions, and better known to many, as that of Saint Paul; countless individuals now turn to the Ouija board for guidance rather than to the Holy Spirit; and the cult of satanism grows by leaps and bounds. In view of such religious regression I can only believe the church errs in attempting to solve her problems by striving to "update" the faith. Her structure may change, but never the gospel.

Many who have left their churches have remarked to me, "The church is dead, and besides, who needs it? All that matters to me is my own personal relationship with Jesus." This is not the Christian faith, for one cannot be a Christian alone. All Christians are together in Christ, members incorporate of His mystical body, which is "the blessed company of all faithful people" (B.C.P., p. 83). We can imagine Saint Paul's reaction had one of his converts come to him and said, "Paul, I believe in the crucified and risen Christ whom you preach—but I don't care to be a member of His body, the church."

The salvation of our own souls is certainly a matter of inexpressible importance, but as Christians we cannot stop there. We cannot be satisfied that we, individually, have accepted our salvation, and live out our lives basking exclusively in the glory of our intimate personal relationship with our Lord. The primacy of the individual at the expense of the body was never the teaching of the ancient, power-filled church. As Saint Paul says, "None of us lives to himself, and none of us dies to himself" (Rom. 14:7). We can only partake of the blessed freedom of God in the measure that we are concerned with the salvation of others. Those who are free in Christ *must* be concerned with others.

"I have become all things to all men, that I might by all means save some," says the apostle (I Cor. 9:22). In his concern for the salvation of others, he even goes so far as to say he would forfeit his own salvation if by so doing he could bring others to Christ (Rom. 9:3).

Frequently I come upon those who are interested only in their own relationship with God, and I know from what I have observed that if we reject the corporate and institutional side of the church, nothing can keep any of us from a narrow intensity; from an overemphasis on certain aspects of the faith; from a basic uncharitableness. The ultimate result of such rejection seems to be inevitably, as Von Hugel says, "a shifting subjectivity, and all but incurable tyranny of mood and fancy: fanaticism is in full sight." [1]

"I will give thanks unto the Lord with my whole heart, secretly among the faithful, and in the congregation" (Ps. 111:1). All over the world, small groups of the faithful are meeting for prayer and study. These groups are a happy compromise between the impersonality of today's large churches and the "lone wolf" Christian. Here deep spiritual needs are met and great spiritual power released. However, these groups should never serve as a substitute for the church, but as a supplement to it.

The ever-increasing number of persons who are turning to the Far Eastern religions are in revolt against today's materialism. They hunger for the mysticism which is actually a part of the Christian heritage; yet the church does not proffer the spiritual treasure she possesses. When she refuses to offer that which is uniquely hers to give, she falls far behind the times because of her very effort to keep up with them. In her tendency to believe that the faith once delivered (Jude: 3) is meaningless and irrelevant today, the church, in my opinion, fails to meet the spiritual needs of her people because she has misinterpreted them. She has sought to feed her people by becoming increasingly secularized, when it is in the field of the spirit that they are starving. It is not good works alone, however important, or new liturgies, however welcome, that will bring the young and not so young back to our churches; it is the evidence that Christ still lives.

[1] Baron Von Hugel, *Spiritual Counsel and Letters*, Douglas V. Steere, ed. (New York: Harper and Row, 1964), p. 132.

At one of the services in a recent healing mission in New York was a girl in her early twenties, obviously a hippie. I was to learn that she attended a Buddhist temple. What then was she doing at a Christian healing mission?

She suffered from a cruel form of arthritis that afflicts the young, and was unable to move without the help of a walker. She had been raised as a Christian but had long since abandoned the faith. Her family's pastor had prevailed upon her to attend the healing service, to which she had agreed out of sheer desperation.

She was marvelously healed that night. The following morning she got out of bed and walked unaided. But the healing of the spirit she received at the altar rail was far more significant than her physical healing, wonderful as it was.

She told me that as she received the laying on of hands, she saw a great blinding light, and she was conscious of a Presence so real she felt it almost palpable. Suddenly she knew Who that presence was, and she called Him by name: Jesus, her Saviour and Redeemer.

The pastor of the mission church knew little of the healing ministry, and he later confessed that he and his wife had discussed the healing of this girl at great length. Why was *she* healed, they wondered, while other long-committed Christians had perhaps remained unhealed?

The answer seemed to me very clear: This girl had been healed that she might go home and tell her friends what great things the Lord had done for her (Mark 5:19). This is precisely what she did, and many of her friends were brought to Christ through her witness.

Then there was the night at Calvary when I found a young man waiting to speak to me after the service. He was a postgraduate student at the University of Pittsburgh, where he led a free-thinking movement. On his way home he had seen the lights in the church, and out of curiosity (and also because he was cold) he had stopped by.

He claimed that the moment he entered the church, he "felt" something he had never experienced before. Just when he had decided it must be his imagination, the laying on of hands began. Something seemed to push him to his knees, and as he knelt alone in a rear pew, he experienced God. He knew beyond the shadow of any doubt the reality of Christ.

It was difficult for the young man to tell me this, and even more difficult for him to say, "I know now I've been on the wrong track. I want to learn all I can about the Christian faith."

For many weeks this young man returned, each time bringing a friend. He is now a Christian leader on campus.

For these young people and the many others like them, the Christian faith is highly relevant; it has changed their lives.

I think of the young woman who had never heard of the healing ministry until two weeks after her husband died. Someone told her of the services at Calvary, and she came, distraught, grief-stricken, frightened, desolate beyond description.

Week after week she came, as we claimed His promise to bind up the broken-hearted (Isa. 61:1), to give that peace which only He can give. We prayed that she might receive the full grace and consolation of His Holy Spirit; that He guide her along the paths He wanted her to walk in, and open those doors through which He wanted her to pass. We watched with awe as God worked in the life of this woman, and we saw her made whole again in Him. What could be more relevant than this?

Then there was the hard-headed businessman who

came to a healing service at Calvary at the instigation of
his wife. He had scheduled a vitally important business
meeting in New York two days later, and he came to
the altar rail asking the guidance and blessing of God.

The meeting was successful beyond his company's
greatest expectation. When he was complimented on how
he had handled the conference, his response was "I
didn't; God did." Ask *this* man whether or not the faith
is relevant.

And what could be more "relevant" to the countless
sick who have been restored to health through the healing ministry? Through this ministry innumerable people
have learned for the first time something of the power
and glory of God. Many for the first time have experienced something of the infinity of His love that is
Himself, who alone can make us and the world whole.
And what can be more relevant than this?

I believe that many and probably most of the world's
problems are spiritually based. Prejudice is one example.
Prejudice cannot be *legislated* out of people, nor can
it be *reasoned* out. It is a spiritual problem. All of us
have some prejudice in some area of our lives, and all
of us need the reconciling touch of Christ upon our
spirits if we are to be healed.

To the extent that we are prejudiced, or greedy, or
bigoted, or hateful, to that extent are we separated from
God and "there is no health in us" (B.C.P., p. 23).
Again, it is the living, healing Christ alone Who can de-
liver us. And in His deliverance we are aware once more
of the eternal relevance of the faith.

Often after a healing service at Calvary someone new
to the services will say, "I plan to come here every
Monday night instead of going to my own church on
Sunday. I've been here three times and I get so much
more out of *these* services."

However happy I am to be told that the healing services are meaningful, such a comment always disturbs me. Everyone is welcome at Calvary, believers and skeptics, the churched and the unchurched. We pray always that the skeptics will become believers, and the unchurched, churched. But those who come to Calvary who are members of a church should never substitute healing services for Sunday worship. However dynamic and important it may be, the healing ministry is only one of the ministries of the church.

To fail to attend church on Sundays is to remove oneself from the worshiping Body. We go to church on Sundays for one purpose alone: to worship almighty God as His people. Our motivation should not be "what we get," but the giving of ourselves. And in the giving, we receive Him whom we worship.

This of course obtains whether or not we are sacramentalists. However, as a sacramentalist myself I am acutely aware of the fact that it is in the congregation of the people of God that the church administers the sacraments. Our Lord said, "Feed my sheep" (John 21:16). Although our spiritual nourishment consists of both word and sacrament, to attend a church where the sacrament of holy communion is offered and claim at the same time to be spiritually unfed seems to me an irreconcilable contradiction.

However imperfect the institutional church may be, she still offers more to her people than any other agency on earth. In my opinion, the church errs if she believes the only way to be meaningful in this era is to concentrate exclusively on social action. Yet this is not to say that she should not concern herself with the world and its problems. Obviously she must, as did Christ Himself, who mingled with drunkards and was Himself accused of being a wine-bibber, who associated with prostitutes and all sorts of undesirable people. He is no less today in and with alcoholics and junkies and hippies.

The church must be found, as is her Lord, wherever there is pain, and this she is making heroic efforts to do. Whatever her faults, complacency is not among them, for she is her own severest critic.

Many spiritually gifted individuals are impatient with what they feel to be the slowness of the church, her failure to keep pace with *them.* Yet on the whole, I have found the church to be a wise mother who recognizes the danger of being "tossed to and fro, and carried about with every wind and doctrine" (Eph. 4:14).

It has become increasingly clear, however, that the church can never again retreat to her ivory tower of aloof "otherness," apparently forgetting that Christ died for all men and that He looks with compassion upon the suffering world. But neither should she over-correct her former position by plunging headlong into almost total secularism, forgetting that she is Christ on earth today doing all that she does in His name; for He is her center, her heart, and her head, still reconciling man to God.

More and more churches are achieving balance by becoming involved in the healing ministry. They recognize in this ministry not only a means of reconciliation, but a powerful instrument of spiritual renewal, by which the Holy Spirit is revitalizing, revivifying, and restoring to the Church her long-diminished spiritual power.

There are those who say the church has failed. While it is true that some of the clergy and laity alike (both of whom comprise the church) have failed—the one to preach the living Christ and the other to hear—the church herself cannot fail. She is the Mystical Body of which we are all members, and Christ the Head (Col. 1:18); she is the Bride of Christ, and as such, one with Him (Rev. 21:2); she is the risen Christ among us, and Christ can neither fail nor die.

The church has been called a hospital for sinners. We

all need this hospital, for we cannot survive without its care.

The church is the dispenser of the sacraments, without which many of us could not live, nor would we want to.

Christ loved and for which He gave Himself (Eph. 5:25),

The church is the household of God (Eph. 2:17–22). We cannot exist as Christians outside the fold of this household.

If we are not members of the body, the church that we cannot call ourselves Christians. And we are not good Christians unless we contribute our prayers and our spirituality, such as it is, to the body, unless we uphold the church of Christ as He, through His church, continually upholds us.

Chapter 18

THE CHARISMATIC REVIVAL

SPIRITUALLY SPEAKING, we are living today in wonderful, exciting, and curiously paradoxical times. On the one hand, many are predicting the demise of the institutional church, while on the other, we are witnessing extraordinary manifestations of the Holy Spirit which bring joy to the heart of every believer. Yet our joy is tempered by the knowledge that from time to time throughout the history of the church there have been comparable periods of holy fire that have flamed through Christendom, only to burn out because of our abuse of the gifts bestowed upon us by the Holy Spirit of God.

These same abuses and excesses are once again becoming all too evident. However, if we are fully aware of the dangers confronting us, there is no reason why the dismal history of the past need be repeated. It is to call attention to these dangers that I write this chapter, in the hope and with the prayer that if we pay heed, we may see in our time the genuine beginning of Joel's prophecy: "And it shall come to pass, that I will pour out my Spirit upon all flesh" (Joel 2:28).

What is known as the charismatic movement has become, in many minds, erroneously synonymous with glossolalia (speaking in unknown tongues). Actually, the charismata applies to *all* the gifts of the spirit as enumerated by Saint Paul in the twelfth chapter of his First Epistle to the Corinthians, of which many are being manifested today.

The apostle makes clear that the Holy Spirit "distributes different gifts to different people, just as he chooses" (I Cor. 12:11 Jer.). In other words, all Christians do not necessarily have all or the same gifts of the Spirit (Rom. 12:6). However, all do have, by virtue of their baptism, the gift of the Spirit Himself.

"Ye shall receive power after that the Holy Ghost has come upon you," our Lord said (Acts 1:8). It is the Holy Spirit *Himself*—the third person of the Trinity—who enables, empowers, and fills us with all joy, not His gifts. The gifts edify and strengthen the church, but they are not essential to her existence; only the Holy Spirit is indispensable.

For years we have neglected the work of the Holy Spirit. We have used His name as a sort of eccesiastical "roger" or sign-off to our prayers. We didn't really know, or think about, just who the Holy Spirit is. The result is that today, with our new knowledge, many of us tend to overreact. For example, a man remarked to me not long ago, "Of course the Holy Spirit is *central*." My reply was a quick "No." He is *not* central; He is co-equal and co-eternal with the Father and the Son, God active in our lives.

The Holy Spirit is the power of the Trinity. He was active in our Lord's earthly life from beginning to end. By His power Jesus was conceived (Luke 1:35); by His power the healing miracles were performed (Acts 10:38); by His power Christ was raised from the dead

(Rom. 8:11). Nevertheless, it is not the Holy Spirit but Jesus Christ who is central to our faith.

"When the Spirit of truth comes he will lead you to complete truth," our Lord says. "He will glorify me since all he tells you will be taken from what is mine" (John 16:13, 14 Jer.).

The neo-Pentecostal movement is now sweeping the established church; and yet this, too, is a misnomer. The true Pentecostal experience is not speaking in an unknown or nonexistent tongue; it is speaking in a foreign language intellectually unknown to the speaker. The Holy Spirit speaks through him to others in their own language so that the Word of God may be understood by the listener.

It was thus on the day of Pentecost nearly two thousand years ago, when those gathered together with one accord in one place "were all filled with the Holy Ghost, and began to speak with other tongues, as the Spirit gave them utterance—and the multitude were confounded, because that every man heard them speak in his own language" (Acts 2:4, 6).

So it was with Saint Francis Xavier, the great sixteenth-century missionary priest. Wherever he traveled in foreign lands, he preached the gospel, and although he had no conscious knowledge of the language of those to whom he preached, he was understood by all. And so it happens occasionally today. A missionary in the Far East, for example, with scant knowledge of the language of the people, immediately upon his arrival begins to preach the gospel fluently and flawlessly in their own tongue. *This* is the real Pentecostal experience.

On that day of the first Pentecost, Peter said, "Repent, and be baptized every one of you in the Name of Jesus Christ for the remission of your sins, and ye shall receive the gift of the Holy Ghost." Then Peter goes on to say, "For the promise is unto you, and to your children" (Acts 2:38, 39); and this means *us*—you and me.

According to Scripture, then, when you are baptized, you receive the Holy Spirit, and thus it is erroneous to regard glossolalia as the sole sign of having received the Spirit of God. Years ago when I talked with the Reverend Dennis Bennett, one of the outstanding leaders in the tongues revival, he was in accord with me that the movement needed a new vocabulary. In his recent excellent book on glossolalia he asks the reader to "please bear with us, and don't be thrown off the track by terminology." [1] Nevertheless, many Christians *are* antagonized on a semantic basis, and one would hope for the evolvement of a more accurate terminology that would allay much criticism of the movement. Even a cursory study of Scripture is sufficient to make apparent this need.

For instance, the phrase "baptism in (of) the Spirit" when referring to speaking in tongues is never used in the New Testament. The apostolic teaching on this point is clear: There are not two baptisms, one of water and one of the Spirit. There is only one baptism. "By one Spirit," St. Paul says, "are we all baptized into one body" (I Cor. 12:13). "There is one Lord, one faith, one baptism" (Eph. 4:5).

To fail to appropriate the Spirit after our baptism, to fail to acknowledge Him, to refuse His leading, are to "quench the Spirit," against which Scripture warns us (I Thess. 5:19). Receiving the Holy Spirit is not a once-and-for-all experience. Every Christian throughout his life should pray for more and more of Him—and as our Lord promises, He shall be given to them that ask (Luke 11:13). Beyond a doubt there is a specific religious experience that for lack of a better name we call the baptism of the Spirit. This consists of a peculiarly vivid infilling of the Spirit, with or without the manifestation

[1] Dennis Bennett, *Nine O'clock in the Morning* (Logus International, 1970), p. 2, footnote.

of tongues. There are continual infillings of the Spirit which may be less dramatic but are nonetheless powerful, so that whatever our task, we are enabled and strengthened by Him to perform it in Jesus' name. The doctrine of the Holy Spirit gradually unfolds in the Old Testament and reaches full development in the New Testament, where since the time of Christ the gift of the Holy Spirit is the gift of the Third Person of the Trinity within the life of every believer—the gift of the risen Lord, given two thousand years ago, and given still to as many as will receive Him, that He may reside in all of us who belong to Christ, controlling and ruling our lives. All who try to follow our Lord, walking in the Spirit as Saint Paul enjoins us (Gal. 5:16), have the valid seal of the Spirit upon their lives.

The phenomenon of glossolalia as it is occurring today has scriptural authority (I Cor. 12:10), and accompanying it is that tremendous joy that comes when there is manifested within us any one of His gifts. No one knows this better than I; however, I can only deplore the fact that the overzealous so frequently equate possession of the Holy Spirit with tongues.

Many have come to me in deep distress because they do not speak in tongues and have been told that they therefore lack the Spirit. This is wholly untrue, and when they say, as did one man who came all the way from California to discuss the matter, "But how can I *know* if I have the Spirit of God?" the answer is "If you manifest in your life the fruit of the Spirit" (Gal. 5:22, 23).

The term Spirit-filled Christian in Pentecostal language means *only* the believer who speaks in tongues, and this is still another error. The evidence of the Spirit-filled believer lies in the fruit and the power of the Spirit, not in the manifestation of tongues. To claim otherwise is unscriptural, for as Anglican priest Michael Harper (who himself speaks in tongues) states, "The only Scriptural

evidence [of the correlation of tongues and the Spirit] we
have at our disposal is a series of incidents in the Book
of Acts, and even this slender documentation is not con-
clusive." [2] Larry Christenson, Lutheran pastor and a
leader in the glossolalia movement, also concedes that a
dogmatic case cannot be made on the basis of New
Testament evidence.[3]

As I see so many around me running from meeting to
meeting frenetically striving to acquire tongues, I am torn
between joy that so many want more of God and apprehension as to *why* they are seeking this particular
gift rather than, let us say, the gift of wisdom. I think
it behooves us all to carefully check our motives. Have
we a sincere desire to strengthen the Body of Christ,
regardless of the cost to ourselves? Or could it be that
we are seeking so frantically simply for our own self-
gratification? Could it be, as I heard one man honestly
state, our desire or what we think is our need to "blow
off steam"? Could it be the weakness of our faith, which
demands a "sign"? Could it be that we seek an emotional "kick" or wish to seem more "spiritual," more
favored by God, than others? The answers to these questions will be given us in quiet prayer.

The gifts of the Spirit are for Christian service and
vary in the faithful according to God's purpose for each
individual; however, *gifts* and *service* are not in themselves evidence of spirituality. The church in Corinth
had the gift of tongues, yet this church was carnal and
corrupt, grossly misusing the gift. This is precisely why
Saint Paul devoted so much space to the subject in
his First Epistle to the Corinthians.

Today the situation in many of our churches is much
the same as at Corinth. Tongues too often have proved

[2] Michael Harper, *Walk in the Spirit* (London: Hodder and Stough-
ton, 1968), p. 20.
[3] Larry Christenson, *Speaking in Tongues, A Gift for the Body of
Christ* (Foundation Trust, 1963), p. 14.

destructively divisive, splitting churches between the "haves" and the "have nots"; and many who speak in tongues are manipulative and spiritually arrogant. In such cases one must conclude that the phenomenon of glossolalia is not always of God. We should never overlook those involved in the charismatic revival who are keenly aware of the abuses within the movement, who are amenable to suggestion and criticism, who are perpetually vigilant against spiritual pride and honestly striving to work within the framework of the church. To such as these, we all owe a debt of gratitude.

As there are dangers in the healing ministry, so there are dangers in tongues: the danger of overemphasis, of seeking the gift rather than the Giver, of inducing tongues, thus removing it from the category of a gift of God to a mere psychological phenomenon. There is also grave jeopardy for the emotionally unstable, who avidly seeking the gift, cannot handle it and are often thrown alarmingly from what may be a mild neurosis into a real psychosis. In Christian concern we should be aware of the gravity of this risk; we should always be cautious and not insistently attempt to thrust what for us has proved a blessing upon another for whom it may be a curse and contrary to God's will.

It is natural enough for us who have received any of the gifts to be enthusiastic over our blessing, to want not only to share our experience but also, in our zeal, to see everyone with whom we come in contact receive the same blessing. This, however, is not within our province, but God's. If we refuse to open our eyes to this fact we are guilty of the sin of presumption and pride, and ours is the guilt of working against the will of God. Far from manifesting the fruit of the Spirit, we may cause irreparable damage to others. This danger obtains with *all* the gifts of the Spirit, all of which are subject to abuse.

There are those, for example, who claim the gift of

healing and refuse to work under the authority of the
church. I know too many such individuals who make the
rounds of hospitals, unasked, and laying hands on a hap-
less patient, say, "Now you're healed. Go home."

If the invalid is very ill and sufficiently gullible to
believe he is healed and leaves the hospital, the chances
are excellent that he will die. If he refuses and happens
to die in the hospital, his family is often assailed by
feelings of intolerable guilt. "If only we had stepped out
on faith," they say in agonized remorse. "If only we
had claimed his healing and taken him home, he would
be alive today."

Then there is exorcism, which is part of the healing
picture. In my opinion, this is dangerous and should
never be done lightly. If time and circumstances allow,
it should be done under controlled conditions. Nor
should it be done indiscriminately, but only if an individual requests it. Yet there are those who habitually
tell anyone who is ill or disturbed that he or she is
demon-possessed. They then proceed immediately, with
no preparation, to exorcise the patient. When he fails to
respond, he now has to struggle not only with illness but
also with the idea that he is possessed. Thus his last state
is infinitely worse than his first.

In many charismatic groups there seems to be an undue emphasis on Satan, an emphasis that culminates in
the age-old heresy of dualism, where Satan and God are
considered co-equal adversaries.

Personally, I find it impossible not to believe in Satan.
But to consider him equally powerful with God, who in
Christ has won the victory, is inconsistent with the
Christian faith. Satan is strong, yes, but he exists by God's
permission, and his power is strictly limited. As he was
overcome by Jesus, so he continues to be overcome as
we call upon the protection of our Lord.

To refuse to acknowledge that Satan exists seems to

me to fall into his trap. To make him the scapegoat for our personal sins is an easy way out of individual responsibility. To concentrate on him equally with and sometimes to the virtual exclusion of God is heresy.

I remember well my discomfiture when I found myself inadvertently participating in a small healing service with someone who seemed greatly overfocused on Satan. We both laid hands on each supplicant, alternating our prayers. Not once did my partner mention the name of God affirmatively: Each prayer dealt exclusively with casting out Satan.

The gift of prophecy likewise is subject to dangerous abuse. I know many with a genuine gift in the New Testament sense of delivering God's message to us today. Yet I know others who claim the gift of prophecy who are doing untold harm. These will say, for example, to one who is very ill, "The Lord told me that on April thirteenth at five in the afternoon, you will be healed."

These self-termed prophets leave in their wake an anguished trail of unfulfillment. The gullible, made so by desperation, are crushed by bewildered disappointment when the predicted healing fails to occur on schedule. Not only should *no one* have the temerity to set dates and times of healing, but no one should ever *promise* a physical healing to anyone.

Someone has said, "The corruption of the best, is the worst," and so it is with the gifts of the Spirit. Those who are peculiarly open to the Holy Spirit are also open to evil spirits—and every gift can be emulated by Satan.

I have mentioned the excesses in those areas that come most often to my attention, and I have seen the damage caused to many lives. I have seen the emotional disturbances, the mental derangements, the harm done the physically sick by the abuse of the gifts. I have seen spiritual pride engendered in the cults that have begun outside the church, because "the Holy Spirit is not op-

erative in our church and certainly not in our pastor.
Therefore we meet at our homes instead, where He
is operative." I have seen countless marriages destroyed
because the partner of the one who has a particular
gift has not the same gift. All these things are particularly heinous because they are done ostensibly in the
name of Jesus.

During the past few years thousands have been blessed
by one or more gifts of the Spirit through which the
church has been edified. However, if the present trend
toward prostitution of the gifts continues, if we fail to
exercise due vigilance, I am fearful that what might
have been an unprecedented and glorious outpouring of
His Spirit upon all flesh may end instead in ever more
ungodly and ungovernable excesses. Then it will be as
Carl Jung has said of the past: "Fanaticism is always a
sign of suppressed doubt. Always in those times when
the Church begins to waver, the style becomes fanatical
or fanatical sects spring up, because the secret doubt
has to be quenched. When one is really convinced, one
is perfectly calm and can discuss one's belief as a personal point of view without any particular resentment." [4]

If we follow as the Spirit of God leads us into all
truth, we will never take our eyes from the Lord Jesus.
If we strive to follow Him, to align our wills with His,
we can come to no harm, nor will we ever harm others
in misguided zeal. We will come to know with Saint
Paul that the greatest of all His gifts is love, the "more
excellent" way of which the apostle speaks (I Cor. 13:1).
Prophecies shall fail, he tells us; tongues shall cease and
knowledge will vanish away (I Cor. 13:8). Only faith,
hope, love, will abide, and the greatest of these is love
(I Cor. 13:13).

[4] C. J. Jung, *Analytical Psychology: Its Theory and Practice* (New
York: Pantheon Books, 1968), p. 172.

Chapter 19

SUGGESTIONS FOR THE LAY PERSON WHO WOULD MINISTER TO OTHERS

THE HEALING MINISTRY is a costly ministry for all who participate in it in any way: for those who seek healing for themselves; for those who intercede for others; for those who minister in any kind of public capacity. It is costly in terms of involvement and selflessness, for it is a fellowship of the truly concerned. At the same time, it can be the most rewarding of all ministries for the lay person.

While love is not confined to the Christian, it is as Dietrich Bonhoeffer says: "Human love is directed to the other person for his own sake; spiritual love loves him for Christ's sake." [1] And so it is with those in this min-

[1] Quoted in *The Little Chronicle,* Oct., 1970, a Society of St. Francis publication.

istry. They who know the healing Christ have a strong desire to take their knowledge and love out into the world, to minister for His sake to suffering friends and neighbors. Almost daily, lay people query me as to how this may best be done. I address myself here to some questions frequently asked.

(1) "How should I approach the sick who may know nothing of, or do not believe in, the healing ministry?"

The thing *not* to do is to assault the patient with your knowledge that Christ heals. If you do this, you are likely to frighten the patient, who will think you know something about his condition which he has not been told; or you will so thoroughly antagonize him that you will never be able to convey your message.

When asked to visit such an individual by believing (or desperate) members of his family, I have found the best procedure is to go quietly into the sickroom, visiting casually and briefly. When it is almost time to leave, broach the subject by asking, "Do you know anything about the healing ministry?"

If the answer is "No," remind the patient that more than one-third of the gospels is devoted to our Lord's earthly healing ministry, and that it is recorded that He healed all who came to Him. Remind the patient that He is the same yesterday, today, and forever (Heb. 13:8); tell him briefly of the early post-apostolic church, in which healing was expected and received; explain today's revival of the church's ministry of healing and mention some of the wonderful things that are happening as a result. If you feel an impulse to pray for the sick person, ask if you may do so. In the majority of cases the patient is delighted. If members of the family are present, suggest that they (and the patient if he is able) might like to do some further reading concerning the healing ministry, and leave with them some pamphlets and a list of books. Suggest to the family that they attend healing services as intercessors.

If you find the patient alone when you visit, offer not only to hold him in prayer during the week but to attend healing services on his behalf, and ask him to be in prayer at approximately the same time. To offer yourself as intercessor, praying that you will be an open channel for God's healing power, is at once a high calling and the sacred duty of all Christians.

If, however, when you ask the patient if he knows anything about the healing ministry he replies, "Yes— and I don't believe a word of it," this is your cue to strike a light note. In such cases I have found it helpful to say something like, "Well, *I* believe in it. I *have* to on the basis of Scripture and what I've seen happen in so many lives." Then I go on, "How about indulging *me*, even if *you* don't believe, and letting me say a prayer with you?"

I have had some amusing experiences with this approach. In one case, for example, a man whose wife had asked me to visit him watched television the entire time I was praying. Nonetheless, this man, who was critically ill, took a dramatic turn for the better two hours later. Healings under these conditions lead to the next question.

(2) "How important is the faith of the person who is ill?"

This question I have discussed earlier in some detail. Suffice it to say here that, while helpful, it is not necessarily essential. However, there must be faith *somewhere*. The man who watched television during the healing prayer may have had little or no faith, but *I*, who was ministering to him, believed. With the very sick we should not demand a miracle-working faith, for this takes an energy they do not possess. Rather should we who believe offer to exercise faith for them.

(3) "Should I lay hands on the sick?"

This is a question which, in my opinion, cannot be answered by a categorical "Yes" or "No." The laying on of hands, while itself not a sacrament, is a sacramental rite, and therefore should not be used indiscriminately by people who have no concept of what they are doing or why; nor should it be received by individuals without some explanation, lest the healing rite be misconstrued as magic. Incalculable harm has been done the healing ministry by those who have great zeal but no knowledge.

It is my belief that those who feel a vocation to lay on hands should do so always under the aegis of the church. In the healing ministry, one is handling the power of God, and this requires emotional balance—a balance that seems to me virtually impossible to maintain without the stabilizing influence of the church. In general, the safest rule to follow is simply to pray, holding the hand of the patient. If the one in need is a member of your own family, by all means lay on hands whether or not you feel you have a "vocation"; for love is the greatest healing force on earth.

(4) "What about ministering to someone who is unconscious?"

Talk and act with him as if he could hear every word you say. Take his hand if you can; explain briefly about the healing Christ, the will of God for wholeness, His power to mend all brokenness. Then offer aloud your prayer for healing.

There have been occasions when I have done this and a nurse has walked into the room. Clearly thinking me mentally incompetent, she has said, "Don't you know this patient is in a coma and can't hear a word you say?" I just nod and go on praying, for there have been numerous times when a patient emerges from his coma days later and remembers every word and prayer that has been uttered. The ears may not hear at the time, but the spirit never sleeps and is never unconscious.

I recall vividly the case of a man desperately ill whom I had visited several times. The man knew his condition, and in talking with me remarked that he had never had an experience of God and was afraid to die. With these words, he lapsed into a coma.

I drew up a chair close to his bed and read to him portions of Scripture. Then I asked the unconscious man to picture our Lord at sundown at the end of a long day. Jesus was very tired, and when He came out from the house in which He was staying, He saw the streets lined with pallets on which lay the sick and dying. Our Lord forgot His fatigue, and in mercy and love He ministered to each and every one, and all were made whole (Luke 4:4).

I spoke a few words about the love God held for the sick man lying in a coma, of how He knew exactly what was happening, and even then stood beside the bed, stretching out His hand to heal. Then I left the room.

The next morning the man's wife called me, her voice jubilant. Her husband had recovered consciousness and had asked to see me. That afternoon I found him sitting up in bed, his face radiant. His first words were, "I experienced the love of God last night. Never have I known such joy and peace." Then he went on to say, "How could anyone knowing this love ever be afraid to die? I know I'm not anymore."

This man did not die; from that day on he made a swift and uneventful recovery. This episode leads into questions concerning death and the healing ministry which are frequently asked, and which we should be prepared to answer.

Not long ago I received a letter from a mother whose little girl had recently died. The person who had ministered to the child before her death had commented that we are with Jesus, whether on earth or in heaven. The mother asked, quite logically, "Why then do we pray for healing on this earth?"

My answer to her, as to all who ask this question, was

to this effect: God has given us life for a purpose, and it is our obligation to seek to preserve that life. We are called to emulate as closely as possible the healing work of our Lord. Therefore we pray for the healing of the sick, following as best we can the example of His ministry of healing set before us in the gospel.

Some time ago I heard a gentleman make a remark I have never forgotten. "If I live," he said, "Christ is with me; if I die, I am with Him." These are the words of someone who knows and loves his Lord. It is the expression of that knowledge universally held by the early Christians which accounts for their joy in the face of death. It is another way of stating Saint Paul's sentiments when the apostle says, "For me to live is Christ, and to die is gain. For I am in a strait betwixt the two, having a desire to depart, and to be with Christ; which is far better. Nevertheless to abide in the flesh is more needful for you" (Phil. 1:21–24).

We pray for healing not because we fear death, but in obedience to our Lord's command to heal the sick; and with the realization that the life we pray for, whether ours or someone else's, may be "more needful" here on earth.

A common question was voiced by a woman recently widowed who said, "I have been told that prayer lengthened my husband's life by at least two years, but during these two years, he suffered greatly. Wouldn't it have been better if we had not prayed, and he had died before he began to suffer?"

To me a question of this kind carries with it the inference that prayer is some sort of magic, or else is offered to change the mind of God. Prayer is not magic, and the mind of God cannot be changed. Had God not willed that this man live two extra years beyond medical expectation, he would *not* have lived; however, had prayer failed to be offered and every effort made to fulfill the primary will of God for him, he might well have died prematurely. There was divine purpose in this extension of life, a purpose we cannot understand, yet I think of the many I have known whose lives have been prolonged far beyond medical possibility. In so many of these individuals I have seen an awe-inspiring spiritual growth.

I think in this connection of a woman with cancer. Had she died three years before she did, she would certainly have been spared much suffering, yet she grew from a nominal Christian to a spiritual giant in those three years. During the last hours of her life she asked her husband if she was dying. He replied, "Yes." She squeezed his hand and whispered, "These past three years have been the most glorious of all our lives together." With this her husband, who had watched her suffer and had suffered with her, concurred.

The mother of a twenty-year-old girl asks a question pertaining to her personal experience.

"Every time I prayed for Helen," she said, "I received the assurance that she would be all right. This impression was so strong that at times I was sure I heard a voice saying, 'Don't be afraid. Helen will be healed.' I claimed this promise," the mother continued, "but Helen was not healed. Why did I receive this assurance when, in fact, she was to die?"

This experience of assurance is not unique. Often the individual is healed here and now as we have prayed; sometimes the healing comes through death. In either case the assurance is valid, and our claim is honored. It is simply that we tend to forget that we are even now living in the midst of eternal life, that we are separated from our beloved dead by only the thinnest of veils—our physical senses. Thus we have mistaken the assurance because we make so vast a differentiation between life and death, when actually life is a continuum, beginning when we come from God, and continuing eternally when we return to Him.

The mother of this young girl asked the inevitable anguished question when the young die: "But why should she have died before she really lived?"

We don't know. Again, although we are certain that it is not God's perfect will that a young girl die of cancer, we cannot be sure that her death itself was not according to His purpose. Much prayer was offered for this beautiful young woman, who came regularly to healing services. We observed the increasing radiance about her and watched her grow in Christ to an awesome degree. Perhaps she died because of the unbelief of the world, the lack of faith of the church universal, our own imperfect prayers. But just perhaps she had fulfilled her purpose here on earth, for she touched and inspired countless lives in her own so-brief one. All of us who knew her grieved for her family and for ourselves; for her we could know only joy that she was now fully with her Lord, whom she so greatly loved.

One of the great joys of the healing ministry to me is that those who know the healing Christ are unafraid to die. They go to meet their Lord with joy, knowing that His *is* the "greatness, and the power, and the glory, and the victory" (I Chron. 29:11).

For those left behind, there is much suffering; but the anguish is eventually transcended by the triumphant knowledge that the one they love is now wholly with Christ, in whom lies the final victory.

Chapter 20

"WHOM SAY *YE* THAT I AM?"

A CERTAIN DAY stands out clearly in my memory, because within the space of a few short hours great truths of the healing ministry were capsulated.

It began on a Sunday morning when I had an appointment with a theologian who was coming from many miles away to discuss the ministry of healing. I had just returned from early church when the doorbell rang and I ushered in the distinguished-looking and very dignified middle-aged man with whom I was to spend the next three hours.

At the end of ten minutes of conversation I knew him to be a brilliant and immensely complicated individual. At the end of fifteen minutes it was evident that he had not in reality come to "discuss" the healing ministry, but to tell me his story and ask my advice and prayers for healing.

Some months before, he had undergone an extremely traumatic personal experience, which had led him into an interest in the ministry of healing, about which he had known virtually nothing until that time. When I saw him, he was in a state of great emotional conflict, and doubtless as a result of this had developed a severe physical disability. The latter, however, was the least of his concerns at the moment.

A scholar with an outstanding mind, he realized that his intellect was a stumbling block. He was aware that he lacked the simplicity of faith generally required of us if we are to receive the healing power of God.

As he talked, I listened carefully with my physical ears to what he said, and equally carefully with my spiritual ones for the guidance of the Holy Spirit. It was abundantly clear that God would have to be the counselor, not I, for from the human viewpoint his problem seemed insoluble.

He talked for over two hours, I said what I felt guided to say, and then we prepared for prayer and the laying on of hands. The entire situation was so complex that the man was unable to state precisely what he wanted prayer for, nor did I of myself have the remotest idea how to pray. With the supplication that the Holy Spirit pray in me according to God's will, we began. In the middle of the healing prayer, the presence of God was so overwhelming that I was forced to my knees. Necessarily removing my hands from his hand, I actually saw the hands of Christ replace mine. At that instant, the man began to pray in an undertone along with me. I was quite certain that he had never prayed in that manner before.

Suddenly laughter and joy, which seemed to emanate from the innermost depths of his being, began to erupt in this man. At the end of the prayer, he rose from his knees, thanking God, laughing and crying at the same time. Again and again, with what I sensed was for him unprecedented abandon, he exclaimed, "Praise God!" And then he said, "It is all so *simple*. At last I can see that He can take care of the entire situation. *He* is now in control, and there is nothing I have to do except praise and thank Him."

This man had a real conversion experience, and both he and the brokenness in his life were healed. As a corollary, his physical ailment had instantaneously disappeared.

His words, "It is all so simple," have stayed with me. Time and again I have emphasized that the healing ministry is not *easy*, for it is incredibly difficult for most of us to become again as little children. But *simple* it is, and this man, by the grace and touch of the Lord Jesus, had been able to discard his intellect, and becoming again as a little child, had been converted (Matt. 18:3). For the very first time, he knew what the joy of the Lord really meant; not because he had been healed, but because he had experienced God.

God is giving us—and the world—a choice. "Come unto Me," He says, "and you shall be endued with peace and power." Or, "Go your own way and destruction will be wrought—not by Me, as an act of vengeance—but by yourselves, who are voluntarily choosing the hell of your own making instead of the heaven of Mine."

Our choice depends upon our individual response to the question He asked of His disciples two thousand years ago and continues to ask of each of us today: "Whom say ye that I am?" (Matt. 16:15).

Many who before could not answer this question with certitude have come through the healing ministry to echo with grateful hearts the reply of Simon Peter: "Thou art the Christ, the Son of the living God" (Matt. 16:16), the Christ who cures the sick, heals all suffering, and binds up the wounds of the broken-hearted.

When we say and mean, "Thou art the Christ," we open our hearts to the love and enabling power of the living God within us. We open our hearts to the transcendent God, Who directs and rules our lives. We see

His hand in all the blessings of this life, both great and small.

"Whom say ye that I am?" The Christ, the Son of the living God; He who dwells in me and I in Him. He, as Saint Paul says, "who was crucified through weakness, yet liveth by the power of God" (II Cor. 13:4). He whose touch is upon me and my life; He who is responsible for everything I do which is good, for every breath I draw. He of whom I am somehow conscious every time I walk across the room; He who governs and plans my life if only I will listen and obey; He who forgives and loves, no matter how great my transgressions. He who guides my every faltering step along the road to holiness—that incredibly difficult path I could never travel alone. He who raises me each time I fall; He whose light shines in the darkness, illumining the narrow way I seek to tread and the strait gate that lies ahead. He who finally picks me up in the everlasting arms and carries me through, so that at the last I am wholly with Him whom I worship and adore and fervently long to praise and serve throughout eternity.

"Whom say ye that I am?"

Thou art the Christ, the Son of the living God; the Saviour of the world who by Thy Cross and Precious Blood hast redeemed and saved us.

This is the Christ whom I love beyond this world; the Christ who died for me; the Christ who carries my burdens, who suffers with me so that I am never alone. Thus the yoke of this life becomes easy and the burden light in Him.

"Whom say ye that I am?"

Thou art the Christ, the Son of the living God; the Lord of great pity and tender mercy (James 5:11), whose promises I have claimed, and so know that He is faithful.

"Whom say ye that I am?"

Thou art the Christ, the Son of the living God: Light of Light, Very God of Very God, of whose kingdom there shall be no end.

We have made our irrevocable choice; for "He who commanded the light to shine out of darkness, hath shined in our hearts, to give the light of the knowledge of the glory of God in the face of Jesus Christ" (II Cor. 4:6).

Afterword

To be a Christian is an exciting and wonderful thing, and I think we don't sufficently realize how immeasurably blessed are those of us who claim the Christian faith.

It is what we *are* (the fruits of which are how we live and what we do) that makes us Christians. And what we are is what God has made us to be by a special act and how we fulfill this act in our own lives. What is this act? According to the New Testament, it is incorporation into the human nature of Christ, by which His life is communicated to us. We are re-created in Him, for "if any man be in Christ, he is a new creature" (II Cor. 5:17).

As vital members of the Mystical Body, we are empowered by prayer and sacrament. As Saint Thomas Aquinas has said, these are the means by which we love God in act, so that the divine love may communicate itself to us, and through us, to the world. If we fail to take Christ, who is the embodiment of love, out into the world, we dare not call ourselves Christians; for it is only in giving Christ to others that we are able to possess Him ourselves.

172

The divine love can be communicated through us whether we are physically sick or well. I am only grateful that God upheld me when I had to stand, and endowed me with His supranatural strength so that I might keep working in His service according to His will.

My own physical healing is almost, though not entirely, completed. After nearly six years without one day free of pain, it is for me no small miracle to have now many pain-free days; to be able to have friends in for dinner once again; to take walks; to sit up and read until midnight. These are small things of themselves, perhaps, but each is a victory, together making possible a nearly normal life. Long after I am completely well, I shall see in the ability to live a normal, pain-free life a miracle never again to be taken for granted.

I shall always remember the past years with gratitude to God for His never-failing grace—grace received in many different ways, but for me most abundantly through the sacrament of holy communion, which is the supreme unitive experience of God upon which my life depends. As we partake of His Body and Blood and thus receive His life in us, we are made whole, regardless of suffering, by virtue of ourselves offered and Himself received. I am forever grateful to God for His mercy in answering those prayers uttered during countless sleepless nights that by morning I might be able to receive Him in whom lies all life.

I am grateful to God beyond the telling for His patient love in teaching me those things I could have learned in no other way. Among these, I have learned now, experientially, that it is through pain-filled eyes that we see most clearly the Christ who never forsakes us.

I understand, now experientially, the joy of the Christian who, though lacking all else, knows that His Redeemer lives, and that in Him there can never be despair.

I have experienced the love of God in a fuller way, as I have looked with new eyes on that love shining in all its glory through our Lord as He hung on the cross. I see now that He was impaled there not by the nails which pierced His hands and feet, but by the love He bore us all and lived and died to save.

I know now why it is that the fervency with which we embrace the cross determines the extent of our joy.

"These things," Jesus said, "have I spoken to you, that my joy might remain in you, and that your joy might be full" (John 15:11). I have heard "these things," taken them to myself, and my joy is indeed full.